THE IMPERIAL WAR MUSEUM BOOK OF THE DESERT WAR

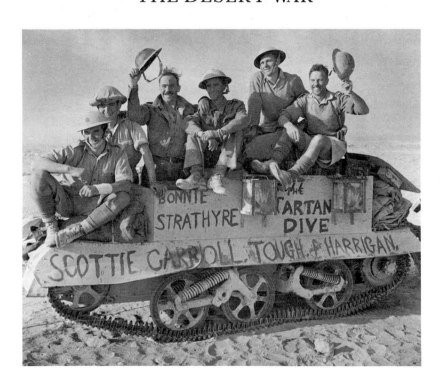

THE IMPERIAL WAR MUSEUM
BOOK OF
THE DESERT WAR

ADRIAN GILBERT

SIDGWICK & JACKSON
LONDON
Published in Association with The Imperial War Museum

First published 1992 by Sidgwick & Jackson Limited

a division of Pan Macmillan Publishers Limited
Cavaye Place London SW10 9PG
and Basingstoke

Associated companies throughout the world

ISBN 0 283 06129 4

1 3 5 7 9 8 6 4 2

A CIP catalogue record for this book is available from
the British Library

Designed by Peter Ward
Maps by DP Press Ltd
Typeset by Parker Typesetting Service, Leicester
Printed and bound in Great Britain by
Butler and Tanner Limited, Frome and London

Contents

Foreword

The Desert War from 1940–42 was a very significant and ultimately decisive episode in the history of the British Commonwealth and Empire. *The Imperial War Museum Book of the Desert War* first and foremost displays the exceptional fighting qualities of those who took part, in this campaign on land, sea and air, from Britain, Australia, New Zealand, South Africa, India and elsewhere; a testament to their courage, resilience, professionalism – and humour. Descriptions are vivid and the variety of experience included exceptional. The book culminates in an inspiring account of the great battle of El Alamein of the which the great war leader Winston Churchill wrote in his book *The Second World War*: 'It may almost be said that before Alamein we never had a victory and after it we never had a defeat.'

Adrian Gilbert, assisted and encouraged by the relevant departments of the Imperial War Museum, has done an excellent job in the compiling and editing. He has been given full access to the riches of the Museum's reference departments and has drawn in particular on the extensive collections of unpublished diaries, letters and memoirs that are held in the Department of Documents. These range from the papers of Field Marshal Viscount Montgomery of Alamein, the victor of that great battle, to the jottings and recollections of front line soldiers.

I hope that this book will be treasured not only by participants in the Desert War but by all those interested in obtaining the authentic feeling of the campaign, of the fighting soldiers at the front and on leave, and also a new insight into a most important phase of military history and indeed of the struggle for survival of the free world.

Field Marshal Lord Bramall KG, GCB, OBE, MC, JP
Chairman of the Trustees of the Imperial War Museum

Preface

This book is an account of the desert campaigns in North Africa, using the resources of the Imperial War Museum. It is not intended as a campaign history; rather, it seeks to illustrate some of the more important or interesting aspects of the war as seen and experienced by those who were there. My role has been to trawl through the mass of documents and interviews held in the Museum and present them within a straightforward narrative framework.

I have divided the book into four main parts. Each part is introduced by a chronological narrative of operations, followed by separate sections which cover subjects of related interest. In addition, there are individual parts on the naval and aerial aspects of the Desert War.

The authoritative help freely given by the Imperial War Museum has been invaluable and to the Museum staff I owe a debt of gratitude. Christopher Dowling, Keeper of the Department of Museum Services, and Neil Young of the Research and Information Office were most helpful in guiding me round the many departments housed within the Museum. It would be almost impossible to acknowledge individually the assistance provided by the Museum staff and so I would like to thank them through the keepers of the respective departments: Angela Weight (Art), Roderick Suddaby (Documents), Jane Carmichael (Photographs), Gwyn Bayliss (Printed Books) and Margaret Brooks (Sound Records).

From the Commonwealth I must acknowledge the help from the Queen Elizabeth II Army Memorial Museum in New Zealand and the Historical Research Section of the Australian War Memorial. A full list of accounts from the Australian War Memorial can be found in the Index of Contributors.

I would also like to thank William Armstrong of Sidgwick & Jackson for his aid in originating and developing the project, Peter Ward for his excellent design, and Lord Bramall for contributing a Foreword to the book. And, as ever, I would especially like to thank Sally Payne.

Finally my main debt of gratitude must be extended to the real 'authors', whose diaries, letters, memoirs and subsequent interviews form the core of this book. Their names can be found in the Index of Contributors at the end of the book, along with other copyright holders who have kindly allowed their material to be published here.

Adrian Gilbert, 1992

Introduction
The Desert War

Fought across the wide expanses of Egypt and Libya, the Desert War was characterized by short bursts of violent action followed by longer periods of relative calm as each side sought to rebuild its forces in preparation for a next round of fighting. In spite of the open terrain and the mobility of the armies this was a strangely indecisive conflict. Ultimately its resolution lay not on the battlefield but through the transformation of the wider strategic picture. Important though the battle of Alamein was, it was the Anglo-American Torch landings in Morocco and Algeria that confirmed Montgomery's victory as one of the war's turning points.

The character of the desert campaigns owed much to their geographical setting. Extremes of climate and terrain were matched by those of distance: Tripoli and Cairo – the respective HQs of the Axis and British – were over 1200 miles distant and, apart from the coast road, communications were poor. While these open spaces enabled an enterprising commander with a mechanized army to engage in a war of manoeuvre his opponent could do likewise. Thus bold advances could be offset by well-managed retreats.

Material factors also tended to cancel each other out. The Axis possessed the advantage of shorter supply lines, directly across the Mediterranean, while their opponents were forced to go the long way round the Cape, but British aircraft and submarines operating from Malta wreaked havoc with Axis convoys – seriously reducing the operational ability of Rommel's forces in North Africa.

At the military level, Rommel and the Afrika Korps held a distinct qualitative edge over the British Army. This advantage, however, was largely negated by the poor performance of the Italians. On the ground, British and German troops both displayed a high standard throughout the Desert War – a tribute to the fighting prowess of each nation. Weapons and equipment were broadly similar in type and performance, the slight German advantages in tanks and anti-tank guns countered by greater British numbers.

These various factors led to a strategic pendulum where a rapid advance in one direction was followed by an equally rapid retreat in the opposite direction. For the British this strange military phenomenon became known as the Benghazi stakes – or the Msus gallop, Agedabia handicap, or other such equestrian metaphor – as the Eighth Army raced backwards and forwards across the bulge of Cyrenaica. To the armchair strategists back in Britain with their maps and flags it was a most disconcerting war to follow; to the men on the ground it was heartbreaking, when the victory promised by a hard-won battle was suddenly transformed into headlong retreat.

As the victorious army advanced along the coast so its supply lines grew longer. Pushing hard to keep contact with the retreating enemy, the victor's troops and equipment became progressively exhausted. Unless captured enemy supply dumps could sustain the advance, logistical breakdown almost inevitably ground the advance to a halt. For the defeated army the process operated in reverse. As the troops fell back towards their home bases so they grew stronger, absorbing supply dumps and incorporating reinforcements rushed up from the rear. In the air (and to a lesser extent at sea) the same moderating influence applied: the further an army was from its home-based airfields the more air cover waned; the nearer it was so it increased. After a period of rest and readjustment the whole process would start up again.

In summary, the first major swing of this strategic see-saw was the Italian invasion of Egypt in September 1940, countered by Wavell's Offensive of December 1940 which flung the Italians back across Cyrenaica. After the arrival of German troops in North Africa, Rommel launched his first offensive in April 1941, ejecting the British from Cyrenaica to a defensive line just inside the Egyptian border.

After a period spent building up reinforcements the British launched a major offensive in November 1941 (Operation Crusader) which, after much hard fighting at Sidi Rezegh, wore down Rommel's armoured strength, forcing him to retreat back to his original starting point. In February 1942 Rommel again advanced from his sally port of El Agheila and drove the dispersed British forces back to the Gazala line, a midway point in the desert continuum. Following a short pause the Axis forces struck with the greatest vigour at the end of May 1942, inflicting a massive defeat on the Eighth Army at Gazala, capturing Tobruk and throwing the British back deep inside Egypt to Alamein, only sixty miles from Alexandria. There the line stabilized, the Axis forces exhausted by their efforts.

Under Montgomery, a greatly reinforced Eighth Army first won a significant defensive engagement at Alam Halfa, then in October 1942 launched a major offensive against Axis positions at Alamein, eventually forcing the Axis to retreat back to Libya. In the light of two previous 'failed' victories the British follow-up was slow and systematic in order to prevent any surprise German counter attack. Fortunately the British were helped by two outside factors. Firstly, unlike those of Wavell and Auchinleck before him, Montgomery's army – on the point of exploiting battlefield success – was not deprived of its best troops to support operations in other theatres of war. Secondly, the Anglo-American Torch landings made it imperative that Rommel retreat to a central position in Tunisia. A resumption of the Desert War had now become impossible.

Seen from the heights of grand strategy – and from hindsight – the course of the Desert War may have seemed inevitable, but to the hundreds of thousands of men of the Western Desert Force and later the Eighth Army it comprised a series of long, drawn-out campaigns punctuated by bewildering and bloody engagements. And if the traditional tenacity of the British soldier had been found wanting then the pendulum would in all likelihood have swung permanently the way of the Axis – with disastrous results for the Allied cause.

*

The British Army has always been a mixed force and the army in the desert was no exception. As well as the troops from the United Kingdom there were substantial contingents from the Commonwealth and Empire, in particular from India, Australia, South Africa and New Zealand. Their experiences form the basis of this book.

Most of these accounts were never intended for publication. They reflect the thoughts and preoccupations of soldiers involved in a great conflict and what they lack in literary polish they make up for in a refreshing honesty and directness.

The memoirs, reports, diaries, interviews and letters assembled here deal with the everyday matters of existence in arduous and at times dangerous circumstances. Shortages of water, the monotony of tinned food, the discomfort of sandstorms, the dangers of aerial attack – rather than deliberations on strategy and tactics – are the concerns of the desert soldier. As in all armies there is a great deal of grumbling, yet alongside this is the fresh enthusiasm of men suddenly set down in a strange, exotic new world, whether it was in the awe-inspiring emptiness of the desert or the turmoil of the great cities of Cairo and Alexandria. The story of their war is graphically told in the succeeding pages.

Quotations The text includes many direct quotations from written documentary material and interview tapes. These are reproduced verbatim whenever possible, but obvious errors have been corrected and minor confusions clarified. It has not been thought necessary to indicate where quotations have been abridged.

Illustrations All the illustrations used in this book have come from the Imperial War Museum, and have been listed with their reference number after the appropriate caption.

The Desert War
A Chronology

1940

10 June Italy declares war on France and Britain.

13 September Italian forces invade Egypt; three days later the advance comes to a halt at Sidi Barrani.

9 December British offensive in the Western Desert opens; the Italians fall back in disarray.

17 December Sollum falls to the British.

1941

5 January Australian troops capture Bardia and take 40,000 Italian prisoners.

22 January Tobruk is captured by British and Commonwealth forces.

7 February The main body of the Italian Army is cut off by British armour at Beda Fomm. Altogether approximately 130,000 Italians are captured in the two-month offensive.

12 February Rommel arrives in North Africa to prepare the way for a German force to support the Italians who have collapsed in the face of the British advance.

20 February British and German patrols make contact for the first time around El Agheila.

31 March Rommel's offensive against the British in Cyrenaica is launched. The British are forced back.

10 April Advance elements of the Afrika Korps reach Tobruk but are unable to breach its defences. The port is cut off three days later.

27 April German troops occupy Halfaya Pass, while the British retire across the border into Egypt.

15 May British launch Operation Brevity to retake Halfaya Pass but the assault is repulsed.

15 June Operation Battleaxe, a British attempt to relieve Tobruk, begins. The initial British advance is easily contained by the Germans who mount a counter-attack and throw the British back to their start line.

5 July Auchinleck formally replaces Wavell as Commander-in-Chief in the Middle East.

12–18 August A series of night convoys relieves part of the Australian 9th Division in Tobruk, replacing them with Polish troops.

18 November Operation Crusader begins, a major British offensive intended to defeat the Axis in Cyrenaica and relieve Tobruk.

19–22 November Confused tank battles take place around Sidi Rezegh, the Germans gaining a slight tactical edge.

23 November The 5th South African Brigade destroyed as a fighting unit south-east of Sidi Rezegh. Auchinleck comes up to Eighth Army HQ to take direct command of the battle and despite the difficulty of the British position decides to press on with the attack.

25–30 November Fierce fighting between the New Zealand Division and Axis forces.

1 December Despite heavy casualties the Eighth Army is still a force in being while the Afrika Korps begins to weaken.

8 December Rommel decides to withdraw from the Crusader battle, rather than let his forces face destruction.

10 December Tobruk is relieved. The Axis forces continue their retreat in good order, first to Gazala and then to El Agheila.

28–30 December A swift German counter-attack inflicts heavy losses on the British vanguard.

1942

21 January Rommel opens his second offensive. Reconnaissance reveals that the British positions are lightly held and the Afrika Korps capitalizes on its initial success and pushes forward with great speed.

29 January Benghazi captured by the Germans.

7 February The Axis advance is brought to a halt against the Gazala line, held in strength by the British Eighth Army. There follows a period of quiet as both sides reinforce their positions in preparation for a resumption of hostilities.

26 May Rommel launches his attack on the Gazala line. His panzer divisions sweep around the British open flank, catching them by surprise.

30 May Rommel withdraws his armour into the 'Cauldron'. British attacks are repulsed by the German anti-tank screen while a supply lifeline is cleared through the British minefields and 150 Brigade is overrun.

5 June The British mount their long-awaited attack against the 'Cauldron', which is soundly defeated. Rommel now launches his forces against the disorganized British armour.

13 June The British begin to pull out of the Gazala position.

20 June Rommel directs his forces against Tobruk.

21 June Overwhelmed by the whirlwind German attack the Tobruk garrison surrenders; nearly 33,000 British and South African troops march into captivity and the Germans gain a vast stockpile of supplies and equipment.

25 June General Ritchie is relieved of his command by Auchinleck who takes direct control of the battle.

28 June German troops capture Mersa Matruh, along with large hauls of Allied prisoners and supplies.

1 July The British make their stand on the Alamein position, the opening phase of what becomes the first battle of Alamein – a series of German attacks which are repulsed by the Eighth Army.

22 July Exhausted by their efforts both sides break off the battle.

13 August Montgomery assumes command of the Eighth Army while Alexander replaces Auchinleck two days later.

30 August Rommel makes a last desperate attempt to force his way round the British defences, but the Axis forces are held by the British at Alam Halfa.

6 September The Germans retire to their original start line. Both sides prepare for the next round – a British offensive.

23 October A massive British artillery bombardment opens the battle of Alamein. British infantry batter their way into the Axis defences but British armour is unable to break through. The battle develops into an attritional struggle which the British must win in the end through superior material resources.

27 October Montgomery reorganizes his forces and maintains the battle in the northern sector of the Allied line despite mounting casualties.

1/2 November Operation Supercharge, the next phase of the Battle of Alamein, gets under way. Another heavy bombardment precedes a renewed British attack which finally overwhelms the exhausted Axis forces.

4 November British armour breaks through the Axis lines but already the Germans are retiring back towards Libya. The British pursuit is delayed by shortages of fuel, bad weather and Montgomery's caution.

8 November Operation Torch, the Anglo-American landings in North Africa, is a success.

11 November British units reach the border with Libya.

13 December Rommel decides to pull back from El Agheila, the Axis stop line during the two previous British advances.

25 December British troops occupy Sirte.

1943

23 January The Eighth Army enters Tripoli, evacuated the previous day by the retreating Axis forces.

4 February Advance units of the Eighth Army cross the border into Tunisia, the end of the Desert War.

PART ONE

THE OPENING ROUNDS

'At first light we fired our first shells in anger. Those early rounds gave everyone immense satisfaction.'
GUNNER L. E. TUTT, *Essex Yeomanry*

Wavell's Offensive and the Siege of Tobruk

Egypt, with its Suez Canal, had always been an area of key strategic importance to Britain. The collapse of France and Mussolini's opportunistic entry into the war in June 1940 placed the Suez lifeline in immediate danger. Formerly, Britain and France had combined to put a halt to Italian adventurism in the Mediterranean. But with Britain forced on to the defensive Mussolini judged the time ripe for the further expansion of his empire.

The bulk of the Italian Army was deployed in the colony of Libya, and it was from there that an invasion of Egypt got under way. On 13 September 1940 an Italian force – numbering 250,000 men all told – crossed the Egyptian frontier and marched sixty miles to Sidi Barrani, where it promptly stopped and began digging in.

Despite Italian numerical superiority, General Sir Archibald Wavell, the British Commander-in-Chief in the Middle East, felt that a limited offensive against the Italians was a viable proposition. The British facing the Italians at Sidi Barrani – the Western Desert Force – numbered around 30,000 men: the 4th Indian Division, 7th Armoured Division and Selby Force, under the command of Major-General Richard O'Connor. A slight, quietly spoken man, O'Connor was chosen to lead the fight against the Italians.

Although limited in scope, the planning for the offensive allowed for subsequent development should the opportunity arise. General O'Connor explained the situation in a conversation after the war:

I hoped our raid would be successful and that if it was so we might be able to exploit it. But it was a complicated affair and I couldn't be certain what use we could make of the success we gained. But I was fully prepared, that if we did get a success that we would make full use of it.

Underpinning O'Connor's thinking was his insistence on secrecy, surprise, concentration of effort and belief in the superiority of the men under his command.

The British force carefully moved into position on the night of 8/9 December: the 4th Indian Division was to break through the Italian defences at Sidi Barrani and then press ahead along the coast road; the 7th Armoured Division was to operate on the open southern flank in a series of wide-ranging out-flanking movements that would overwhelm the slow-moving Italian formations. The plan worked perfectly. Taken completely by surprise the Italians fell back in disarray, to be bundled out of Egypt in a matter of days.

Once over the border, the Italian stronghold of Fort Capuzzo had to be reduced. Amongst the attacking force was Gunner L. E. Tutt, a

member of 414 Battery, the Essex Yeomanry. Equipped with 25-pounder gun-howitzers, Tutt's battery was rushed forward. Recalling the action, he wrote:

Our first position on enemy soil was near Fort Capuzzo and we dug in with a real sense of urgency, hastened by some desultory enemy fire. We were nearly frozen to death during the night. We were still in khaki drill and the shortage of transport had meant that essential clothing, blankets, cookhouse equipment and the like had been left behind. We were sited on solid rock, but I genuinely believe that we wouldn't have changed places with anyone.

At first light we fired our first shells in anger. Those early rounds gave everyone immense satisfaction. I think that a sigh went up from the whole Regiment. Like the elderly spinster, we hadn't wanted to die wondering. Because of the speed of the advance there was no protective screen of infantry between us and our targets. Had they wanted to, a very small group of enemy forces could have popped us in the bag without too much difficulty.

Meanwhile O'Connor had been faced with the sudden withdrawal of the Indian Division (its new task to spearhead the invasion of Italian East

Above: The architects of British victory in the first desert campaign, Lieutenant-General Richard O'Connor (left) and General Sir Archibald Wavell, confer outside Bardia, 4 January 1941. (E.1549)

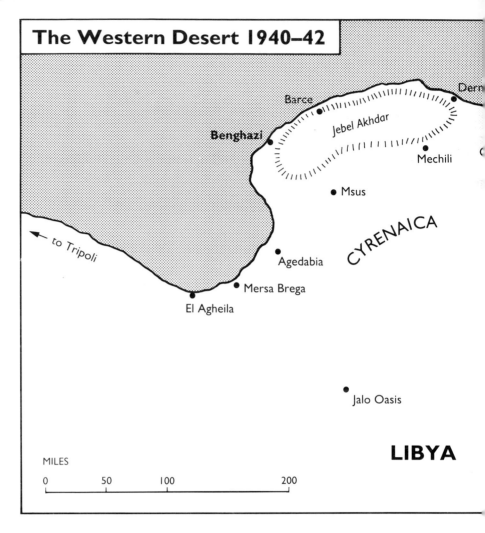

The Western Desert 1940–42

Dern

Barce

Jebel Akhdar

Benghazi

Mechili

Msus

to Tripoli

CYRENAICA

Agedabia

Mersa Brega

El Agheila

Jalo Oasis

LIBYA

MILES

0   50   100   200

Africa) and its replacement by the 6th Australian Division. This change of plan was unknown to O'Connor:

It came as a complete and very unpleasant surprise. General Wavell told me afterwards: 'I purposely didn't tell you because I thought it might affect your operations.' But really, of course, it put paid to the question of immediate exploitation. I don't doubt the desirability, if not the necessity, of those troops being brought to East Africa and Ethiopia. But it all arose from the fact that they didn't expect a big success in the desert and when it did come they weren't prepared to alter their plan.

As a result the Indian Division was replaced by the 6th Australian Division who had never been trained in desert warfare and who had to be re-armed with modern artillery. The net result was that the removal of the 4th Indian Division led to a serious delay before we could attack Bardia and by so doing we lost surprise completely.

Despite the delay imposed upon the British offensive, it continued with renewed fervour following the arrival of the Australians, whose first taste of combat was to be the assault against Bardia on 3 January 1941.

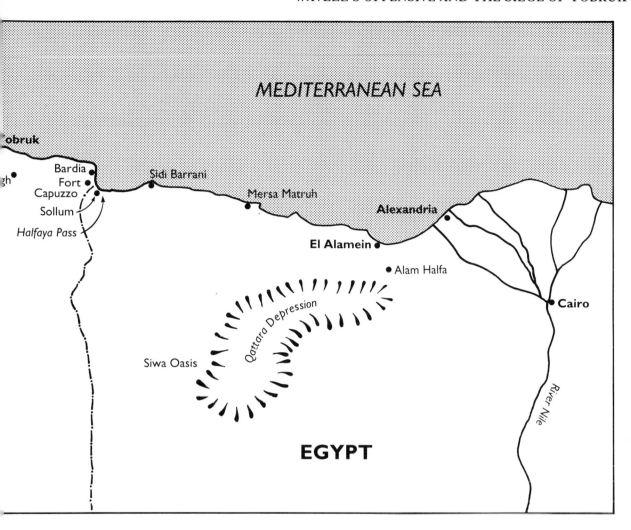

Assigned to provide artillery support for the Australians, L. E. Tutt takes up the story:

We moved our guns to a new position for our attack on Bardia. Details of the assault are more properly documented in the official war diary of our unit, but I have a jumble of impressions of the things that affected me personally. There was the visit of our colonel just before zero hour. His exhortations to battle were so peppered with Tally Hos and talk of flushing out the fox and making a good kill that in the end we were not sure whether to put on our tin hats or our hunting Pinks. I think, had we raised a fox in the course of the battle, we would have lost half the battery after it.

We fired off our first big programme and then moved through the wire surrounding the place to be able to engage fresh targets. We came across a battery of Italians. It became the fashion to decry the Italians as soldiers; this may have been true of their infantry but not of their artillery. In this instance they had died at their guns. Their bodies were scattered close to their firing positions and they must have remained in action until our infantry tanks [Matildas] and the Australians had overrun their gun sites.

Above: British 25-pounder gun/howitzers in action against Bardia. One of the most famous artillery pieces of the war, the 25-pounder was a light yet robust weapon, capable of firing a high-explosive shell to a range of 13,400 yards. (E.1515)

Shortly before this I stumbled upon my first casualty in this campaign. He was an Australian private, new to action because he was dressed in full kit, including a gas mask haversack strapped in position on his chest. A veteran of only a few weeks' active service would have discarded that. I noticed that his rifle was new too; the stock honey colour, unlike our oil-blackened relics of World War One and earlier. It was difficult at first to see how he had died, until one saw the neat, bruise-fringed hole in his temple. He seemed to have assumed heroic proportions in death.

The assault on Bardia would be the Australian 6th Division's baptism of fire. Morale was high and the opportunity of capturing an important enemy position was eagerly anticipated. The War Diary of 16 Infantry Brigade was kept by a former journalist, Corporal R. L. Hoffman:

An intercepted enemy message from Bardia's remaining defenders asked their HQ for all Italian aircraft to come to their assistance. This message asked for 'all our aircraft in Libya'. This indicates desperation and has the imprint of a subordinate's delicate insinuation regarding the lack of assistance.

Corporal H. Rawson was one of the Australian infantrymen who took part in the attack on Bardia. He comments on the textbook style of the advance and the confused nature of the Italian defence:

We had been issued with leather jerkins against the intense cold. In darkness and in an orderly manner the men approached the start line, which was clearly marked with white tape across their front, south of the town. Meanwhile our artillery had opened up and was laying down a barrage while the Navy was firing from offshore.

The 2/1 and 2/2 battalions had gone ahead of us and just before we crossed the start line there was a conference of platoon commanders for final orders. At this stage the Eyeties were sending over a lot of shells and using small arms.

Left: An unusual photograph of an Australian headquarters preparing for the assault on Bardia, 4 January 1941. Despite being new to battle the Australian 6th Division conducted a textbook operation. (E.1540)

Some high explosive landed among our positions and caused casualties. It wasn't that the fire was so accurate as heavy. They couldn't help hitting something.

It was about daybreak when the battalion crossed the line. It seemed like another stunt. There was good discipline among the men and no bunching or crowding. We went at a steady walk. The CO (Lieutenant-Colonel V. T. England) seemed to be everywhere, standing on his carrier, with a balaclava over his head, smoking a pipe. There were still plenty of shells and we had to take cover for a while. When we got near the first line of wire and saw the holes cut by the engineers, there was much confusion. Eyetie prisoners were trying to get through to our lines and our men had to go through to attack. I have never seen such fear marked on the faces of those prisoners. Of course we abused them for holding us up. There was moderate small-arms fire coming our way too, and that didn't help. Not long after this we encountered an artillery post but it didn't give us much trouble. When we got close they didn't seem to worry about fighting but kept in their slit trenches. The crew came out when grenades were thrown among them.

The only other resistance our company met was from a machine-gun nest behind a built-up earthworks. That kept us down for a time. We took cover and decided what to do. The section leader gave an order to charge, but before we got very far a row of white flags went up as if by signal. The gunner in the centre had apparently been shot in the head and when he was killed the others surrendered. We found several other flags in the weapon pits ready for use.

About this time a few Eyetie tanks approached B Company lines. They were engaged by anti-tank rifles and one was stopped although I don't think disabled. Before the position got very bad a formation of British Matildas arrived on the scene and the others were dispersed. We then crossed the Fort Capuzzo Road and shortly afterwards came on a deserted battalion headquarters. Here the men found hot coffee, food, tins of bully beef and medical supplies.

The company began to bed down there for the night. It was very comfortable after our slit trenches. There were well-made dugouts and numerous blankets. Sometime before midnight the Eyeties made a counter attack, consisting mainly of slight but accurate sniping. One of our men who carried dixies in his haversack on his back had them riddled by bullets. Another had his leather jerkin ripped. In stopping the sniping the Northumberland Fusiliers [attached to the Australians] gave an impressive demonstration of concentrated fire. Early on the morning of 4 January we were ready to continue our advance.

As the lines of Italian prisoners trudged out of the fortress, Corporal Hoffman gave this example of theatrical Italian behaviour and a typical Australian response:

Fascist flamboyance was exhibited by a captured major in a column of prisoners. When it had reached a safe spot he rushed to the head of the column and bearing his chest to them, cried (in Italian): 'Shoot me ... and save my honour'. This brave Roman exhortation must be read with the obvious knowledge that whatever the prisoners had, they certainly had nothing with which to shoot anybody. The 'suicidal' major repeated his gesture of honour several times until an Australian sentry approached with a bayonet levelled at the seat of his pants and said: 'Get back, you mug, before I shoot you'. The terrorized Fascist major skipped back into line at the double.

Stretching to the horizon, a seemingly endless column of Italian prisoners wends its way from Bardia to the Prisoner of War cages in Egypt, 8 January 1941. Nearly 40,000 Italians were captured at Bardia – a figure far outnumbering the British and Australian attacking force. (E.1606)

Despite the continuing success of the British on the ground, the Italian Air Force was often overhead, especially during daylight hours. The open terrain of the desert made men and especially vehicles vulnerable to aircraft, but bombing techniques were still fairly primitive and casualties were light. The following two accounts give some idea of the effect of these raids.

Rex Keating, an experienced Middle-East journalist, was responsible for writing and speaking the newsreel commentaries for War Pictorial News and other Allied news operations. During the offensive he had travelled up along the coast in the wake of the British advance:

The following day was a Sunday. And at our forward headquarters everyone was relaxing in the sunshine outside their tents, writing letters, reading and so on. I was chatting with the padre. There was a distant roar of airplane engines and within minutes a dozen or so Italian aircraft appeared. Down they came, circling leisurely over the camp. And off they went. No anti-aircraft guns fired at them. There weren't any. No Allied fighters went up to combat them: there weren't any of those either. 'Well,' said the padre, 'now they've located us they'll be back.'

Sure enough, within the hour, back came a squadron of bombers, unchallenged except for rifles and machine-gun fire. Round and round they flew, leisurely dropping their bombs. We all dived into the nearest slit trench. I was last, on top of the padre, who in turn was on top of a soldier. I was very conscious of the fact that my buttock was sticking up above the trench. The bombs fell all around us. But the only thing I can recall at the time was the incessant flow of bad language from below me. It was in fact the padre.

Dr Theodore Stephanides was medical officer to a Cypriot labour battalion engaged in general engineering duties behind the British advance. Stephanides had been an artillery officer in the Greek Army during the First World War and after the war he set up the first X-ray clinic in Corfu. His interest in freshwater biology led him to meet the young Gerald Durrell (and his writer brother Lawrence), in whose book *My Family and Other Animals* Stephanides figured prominently. Having advanced into Libya, Stephanides and his battalion set up camp:

So far everything had been more like a glorified picnic than a war but I was to see the reverse of the medal that same night. There was a bright moon shining which was almost like a written invitation for the Italian bombers to come over – and soon they did. Just after midnight I was awakened by the shrill whistles of the men on duty as spotters, and almost at once we all heard the planes for ourselves. It was easy to recognize them as Caproni bombers owing to the curious alternating high and low drone produced by their three motors, and we prudently took refuge in a nearby slit trench. Soon the drone was almost overhead and suddenly we were deafened by loud explosions. Stones and splinters pattered around, the ground heaved.

This was my first real taste of the Second World War; and I decided there and then that I disliked bombing even more than the shelling of the First World War. Artillery shells were impersonal but my imagination could never quite get over the feeling that the enemy planes had selected me as their target and that their bombs were aimed at me in particular.

A British Matilda tank of the 7th Royal Tank Regiment; a photograph taken during the early stages of the offensive, 19 December 1940. Designed to act in the direct support of infantry operations the Matilda had a maximum cross-country speed of only 8 m.p.h. but it was one of the successes of the first desert campaign because of its battlefield reliability and its heavy armour which made it virtually invulnerable to Italian anti-tank guns. (E.1416)

After Bardia the next prize to fall was Tobruk, the major port of eastern Libya. Italian resistance was rather stronger than that encountered previously, but on 22 January the town was in British hands. Captain Barker, an officer commanding a troop of Matilda tanks, explains how he dealt with a gun battery on the approaches to Tobruk:

Approaching a wadi we'd been shelled for about three miles without being able to tell where the fire came from. I spotted a gun flash from behind stones on the wadi edge. I ordered my troop to attack, ignoring machine-guns and anti-tank fire from the flank. It was the guns we were after.

Then I heard a whoof of shells passing at point-blank range. It was a question of which would knock out the other first. I just kept straight on and told the gunner to let go when we were near. Although we were yawing and pitching all over the place he hit the emplacement with his first shot.

Then we went for three other guns. I turned quickly, which threw up a cloud of dust, drove round the cloud and took them by surprise. When we were only yards away we could see the men in their dark green uniforms with their coats open, sweating as they tried to hump their guns round and train them on us. We simply went straight towards them, firing; we would have gone straight over them if we hadn't knocked their guns out. Then we drove the loaders and odds and ends into the dugout. And the next thing I saw was a white flag emerging.

Following on directly behind the advance, Dr Stephanides provided this description of his entry into Tobruk:

From early daylight a tall column of smoke, spreading out in a long black cloud when it reached the height of several thousand feet, had been visible to the north-west in the direction of Tobruk. We soon passed the barbed and concertina wire and the tank traps of the Tobruk perimeter and the usual litter of a rout began to appear. Burst open suitcases (these are always seen in a headlong

A vast pall of black smoke hangs over Tobruk harbour following its capture by British and Australian forces. In the foreground are Italian tanks – an M 11/40 (left) and an M 11/39 (right) – now the property of the Australian 6th Cavalry Regiment and painted with distinctive white kangaroo recognition symbols. (E.1766)

retreat), accoutrements, weapons, a few steel helmets, scraps of uniforms and an occasional dead body (usually Italian) which had not yet been cleared up. We passed on our left a huge barbed-wire enclosure swarming with Italian prisoners, and suddenly we topped a small rise and Tobruk and its harbour appeared in front of us.

At first glance – when seen at a distance – Tobruk made a beautiful picture with its flat-roofed, dazzling white houses crowded together on the flank of a low slope overlooking a small land-locked and brilliantly blue bay. What struck me most was the immense amount of Italian shipping sunk in the harbour; masts stuck up everywhere out of the water like pins in a pin cushion.

There was still a bit of fighting, or rather mopping up, going on in the western part of the Tobruk perimeter and we could hear a burst of rifle and machine-gun fire now and then. But all was quiet in the town itself except for occasional shots fired as a *feu de joie* by over-exuberant Australians. We encountered a few of these, together with Italians, waving bottles of wine, singing and exchanging hats – or lying by the side of the road.

The capture of Tobruk did not lessen the momentum of the advance, despite the wear and tear on the British soldiers and their equipment, compounded by a shortage of petrol. Derna fell on 30 January without opposition, the Italians retreating rapidly. O'Connor saw a chance to destroy the Italian Tenth Army in its entirety. If he continued to advance along the coastal plain he would certainly push the enemy out of Cyrenaica, but if instead he sent 7th Armoured Division far into the desert and swung round the mountains of the Jebel Ahkdar he might cut off the disorganized Italian retreat.

Despite shortages of serviceable machines, the 7th Armoured Division drove through Mechili and over the rock-strewn wilderness to Msus and then on to the coast at Beda Fomm by 5 February. There they

An armoured car of the King's Dragoon Guards negotiates its way through the wreckage of Italian vehicles on the coast road at Beda Fomm, February 1941. Beda Fomm represented the culmination of O'Connor's attack, the destruction of the Italian armed forces in Cyrenaica. (MH.3845)

met the first elements of the Italian army streaming south. All the while the Australian infantry were pushing the Italians towards the trap now set at Beda Fomm. Seeing their way blocked on the road to Tripoli – and safety – the Italians tried to break through the barricade of British tanks, but despite a superiority in numbers the attacks were unco-ordinated and failed miserably. The artillery and tanks of 7th Armoured Division reaped a rich harvest of blazing Italian vehicles.

Following the British armour was the celebrated journalist Chester Wilmot, who was well placed to observe the rout of the Italian Tenth Army. Having destroyed forty-six tanks, the British thought there could be little left of the enemy armour that was battleworthy:

After lunch reports came in we could hardly believe. One spoke of 15 medium tanks leading along a transport column. The next reported 25 medium tanks at the rear, and the third said there were 30 mediums interspersed through the column. That made 70 all told but by fast manoeuvring we were able to take them on piecemeal. It was a really hard job, and we fought them all afternoon. By dark there couldn't have been more than 30 left. Nevertheless, by that time more than half our medium tanks were temporarily out of action owing to mechanical trouble, for they had been going without a stop for days. Tanks of one regiment ran out of ammunition twice during the afternoon and had to come back for supplies. Apart from this the fight went on continuously.

The collapse of this last desperate attempt to break through the British grip was followed by white flags as 25,000 Italians gave up the struggle. Altogether the British offensive had advanced 500 miles, destroyed an army of ten divisions and captured over 130,000 men, all for the loss of 500 killed and 1373 wounded. O'Connor signalled Wavell, back at his HQ in Cairo: 'Fox killed in open.'

A photograph of Major G. M. O. Davy, second-in-command of the 3rd Hussars – one of the regiments of the 7th Armoured Division. A keen photographer, Davy took the picture opposite while this photograph was taken with Davy's own camera, hence the empty camera case hanging from his web belt. (MH.3833)

It was a glorious success for the British Army, the first since the opening of hostilities in 1939. Not surprisingly, O'Connor was keen to exploit the victory and by keeping up the momentum of the advance throw the Italians out of North Africa entirely. The demands of the wider strategic picture, however, quashed any hope of a follow-up. Churchill had been pressing Wavell to send troops to support Greece, and now that Egypt was safe from Italian attack the first desert campaign was allowed to fizzle out.

Although disappointed at the decision, O'Connor loyally accepted it without remonstration. After the war he gave his own view on the failure to proceed on to Tripoli:

We completely liquidated the enemy and there were no other troops in the way – nothing to stop us really. I feel that we should have got there; especially looking back in hindsight, after Hitler had said to Rommel of the campaign: 'Don't for one second relax your determination to follow up, whatever the odds; don't be like the British who had a chance of getting to Tripoli and didn't take it.'

As British advance guards carried on along the coast to El Agheila, this first British offensive of the Desert War came to a close. It was unique in character, both sides having to come to grips with the problems of waging war in the wilderness of North Africa. Rex Keating noted that, 'the desert in those early days was very much a comic opera affair'; a view confirmed by other observers. Lieutenant-Commander J. B. Lamb – a Royal Navy beachmaster responsible for landing supplies along the coast – found that at one point, 'liaison with the Army was provided unofficially by a Scots company commander of the Argyll and Sutherland Highlanders who called himself the "King's Harbour Master". He wore an Italian brigadier's uniform with sea boots because none of his proper clothes were in a fit state.'

Dr Stephanides found his men's enthusiasm for sartorial excess even greater. A small-scale battle had ensued when Australian troops had caught the Cypriot pioneers helping themselves to their equipment, fatalities being averted only through the calming intervention of Stephanides and his fellow officers:

Several of our men appeared on parade the next morning in Australian slouch-hats which they thought more becoming than their own fore-and-aft forage caps, and were much surprised and hurt when the hats were confiscated. One of the many little trials of the officers was to get the men to stick to the uniforms that the Army authorities had seen fit to provide them with, and not to dress themselves in whatever caught their fancy – such as a *Bersaglieri*'s plumed hat or the regalia of a Blackshirt colonel.

The Australians were also keen on dressing up. One of Hoffman's entries in the 16 Brigade War Diary on 3 January reads: 'By midday an extraordinary number of our men carried Italian pistols and revolvers at their belts, binoculars round their necks, and some even discarded their own jackets in preference to the gilded majesty of an officer's gold-braided ceremonial tunic.'

Such was the Australian exuberance that the divisional commander, Major-General I. G. Mackay, felt it necessary to issue a communication demanding restraint:

There are indications that civilianism is beginning to break out. Military moves are not being carried out in military ways and military measures are being attempted without due tactical precautions. There is a tendency towards a picnic spirit, evidenced by the promiscuous firing of enemy rifles and pistols and the exploding of bombs, the 'showing off' of units and drivers in possession of captured enemy vehicles, dressing in articles of Italian uniform like clowns and not like soldiers, the collecting of dogs and looking after them instead of men, fraternising with prisoners, and the disinclination of officers to accept responsibility and check these and other tendencies.

The chain of command must be stiffened up. Every leader from the highest to the lowest must regain control and lead.

Another feature of the campaign was the Italian propensity to litter the desert with small anti-personnel mines. Commander Lamb:

The Italians caused a great deal of trouble with their Thermos flask hand grenades, which were everywhere. One afternoon I was surprised by a nearby explosion and looking round saw a drifting haze and a figure on the ground. It turned out to be a Thermos bomb about which an aircraftman had been unduly inquisitive. These bombs, painted an attractive chromium and red, resembled Thermos flasks and were rendered live by impact with the ground. As a rule, they became so sensitive that a good look would almost set them off.

Stephanides often found himself treating his pioneers for Thermos flask bomb wounds but this did not stop him from indulging in some practical joking:

A few days previously, my batman had broken a real Thermos flask of mine and this gave me the idea for one of those childish jokes that military life seems to foster in even the most serious minds. I filled the flask with sand to give it weight, whittled a piece of wood and covered it with tin foil to represent the fuse end, and made the whole thing look like a Thermos flask bomb. The following morning I strolled into the store tent, which was also used as a mess, whilst breakfast was on and with a gay 'Just look what I found outside' dumped the transmogrified Thermos flask onto the table. I never saw a tent empty itself so quickly! I then made myself scarce till lunch time to allow emotions to cool down a bit. The joke caught on with a vengeance and that Thermos flask did the rounds of all the camps in the neighbourhood and, for all I know, perhaps continued doing so until the end of the campaign.

The Italian disaster in Cyrenaica had forced Mussolini to swallow his pride and accept German offers of direct military help. On 12 February 1941 *Generalleutnant* Erwin Rommel arrived in Tripoli, a panzer commander who had made his reputation in the Battle for France in 1940. Following him were advance elements of what was to become the famed Afrika Korps, 15th Panzer Division and 5th Light Division (later renamed 21st Panzer Division). To the consternation of his slow-moving and slow-thinking Italian allies, Rommel instigated an immediate reconnaissance in force.

The first clash with the British took place on 24 February and their negative response convinced Rommel that the time was ripe for an all-out offensive. The British position in Cyrenaica was more vulnerable than it seemed at first sight. The experienced units of Wavell's Offensive had been replaced by troops new to combat; the 6th Australian Division had been exchanged for the 9th Australian Division and the loss of 7th Armoured Division was in no way compensated for by the

A German PzKpfw I light tank moves out through El Agheila in the opening stages of Rommel's offensive, March 1941. In the background are two wrecked British lorries, victims of the speed of the German attack. (MH.5549)

Australian troops hold a forward defensive position as the Germans begin their investment of Tobruk. The exposed, flat terrain forced the troops to dig in and during the course of the siege extensive field fortifications were built. (E.4795)

arrival of 2nd Armoured Division – seriously under strength and lacking in knowledge of desert conditions. The new British commander, Lieutenant-General Philip Neame, also failed to measure up to his predecessor.

Supported by the Italian mechanized Ariete Division the newly formed Afrika Korps struck on the 24 March. The British fell back in disorder. Capitalizing on British disarray, Rommel pressed his advantage and raced forward along three axes of advance, further confusing his opponents. In order to avoid encirclement the British rapidly gave ground and retreated to Gazala, but this did not prevent the capture of Generals Neame and O'Connor (the latter had been sent up to advise Neame as the situation deteriorated). The staff car containing Neame and O'Connor was intercepted by a German patrol near Derna on 7 April. O'Connor's capture was a great loss to the British cause, although his wry comment on the incident was typical:

It was a great shock and I never thought it would ever happen to me; very conceited perhaps but it was miles behind our own front and by sheer bad luck we drove into the one bit of desert in which the Germans had sent a reconnaissance group, and went bang into the middle of them.

The fast-moving armoured columns of the Afrika Korps ran rings around the British who alternately made last-ditch stands or raced back towards Egypt. L. E. Tutt's battery had been part of the line of British troops which had experienced the full weight of the German attack around Mersa Brega on 1 April:

Our battery position was shielded by some low hills. We saw [German] tanks coming over them, wireless aerials with pennants atop like a field full of lancers. They assumed hull-down positions and blasted the thin screen of recovered tanks which were deployed to face them. The men of the Tower Hamlets went forward to face them in Bren carriers and were virtually destroyed in a matter of minutes; their bravery was unquestioned but they should never have been asked to face such odds. Both our batteries fired a heavy concentration on the German Mark IIIs and some Mark IVs and they were forced to withdraw slightly, but it was only a temporary respite as their infantry moved against the flank exposed by the withdrawal of the Free French.

Fortunately the Northumberland Fusiliers turned up with their heavy machine-guns and plugged the gap, allowing us to withdraw and regroup – otherwise we might have ended our contribution to the war there and then. The Fusiliers had a most fearsome reputation. The unit was made up of hard, uncompromising men of little polish; they obeyed their own officers but treated anyone else in authority with contempt, particularly base depot personnel. They were the dourest fighters we were to meet in a long day's march and we were always glad to have them about.

It was dark by the time we were able to disengage from the enemy. Once we pulled out of our positions the rot seemed to set in. We dropped into action a little way down the road but had hardly surveyed the position-in before we were ordered to withdraw again. There seemed to be no overall direction. Too many units were on the move at the same time, a mistake which contributed to a growing panic. The impression was given that the enemy armour was just around the last bend, when in fact they were nearly an hour behind us.

The vast stream of vehicles on the road and either side of it pressed on and we soon saw the danger signs of men abandoning a stalled truck and running to get on another vehicle, when possibly a few seconds under the bonnet would have kept it going. Others were abandoned because they ran out of petrol, and yet there were three-tonners loaded down with the stuff passing on either side.

Had the Stukas come on the massed vehicles, they would have had a field day. One very odd thing did happen. A whole squadron of enemy bombers appeared over a hill and carefully cruised the whole length of the column. They were just above our heads and we could see the pilots grinning down at us. We could not leave the road because of the press of vehicles. Quite clearly, had they wanted to, they could have blasted us off the face of the earth. Probably they had exhausted their bomb load elsewhere and the low flight over our column was an exercise in propaganda showing us that they were masters in the air as well as on the ground.

Eventually Tutt and his unit withdrew into the comparative safety of the Tobruk perimeter, but ever the proud Yeomanry gunner he concluded his account of the retreat: 'The regiment acquitted itself well. We showed none of the blind panic that some of the other formations did.'

The Afrika Korps surrounded Tobruk on 11 April and Rommel immediately ordered an all-out assault in the hope of gaining the port before the British had a chance to organize a proper defence. The attacks failed and the Axis forces had to set about mounting a conventional siege operation, and so began the epic 242-day investment of Tobruk. Under the command of the tough Australian Major-General

Major-General Leslie
Morshead, GOC of the 9th
Australian Division during
the siege of Tobruk.

Leslie Morshead (nicknamed 'Ming the Merciless' by his men) the garrison of Tobruk was a mixed force comprising Australian infantry (the 9th Infantry Division plus an extra brigade) supported by British artillery and engineers plus a few Matilda tanks from the Royal Tank Regiment. It was to be a potent combination.

The Australians and British meshed well together from the outset. Harold Harper, an NCO from the South Notts Hussars (an old Yeomanry cavalry regiment converted to 25-pounder gun-howitzers as the 107th Field Artillery Regiment), recalled his relations with the Australians during the siege: 'On more than one occasion we rescued them from a difficult situation and they took us to heart. Because our cap badge was unlike the normal Royal Artillery badge – it was in the form of an acorn – they called as the Acorn Gunners, and the name stuck for the rest of the war.'

Two further accounts reveal the desperate nature of the fighting in the early phase of the siege, when the perimeter lines were still far from solid. An Australian sergeant talks about his role in repulsing the major German attack on the night of 13/14 April:

Corporal J. H. Edmondson,
who won a posthumous VC
during the fighting of 13/14
April.

When we got back to Tobruk we were told that our posts must be held at all costs. That even if tanks broke through we were to hang on and wait for the enemy infantry. We soon had a chance of testing out these tactics. On 13 April – after dark – enemy infantry got through our wire about 100 yards to the left of the post I was in.

They opened up on us but we were unable to challenge them by fire. So our patrol commander Lieutenant Mackle led a fighting patrol which drove them back at the bayonet. He took with him Corporal Edmondson and five others. They charged the enemy in the face of heavy machine-gun fire and Edmondson was mortally wounded but he kept on and bayoneted two Germans and then saved Mr Mackle's life by bayoneting two more who had Mr Mackle at their mercy. Edmondson died but he was honoured with a VC.

Those enemy who escaped were driven back through the wire. But for this they would probably have surrounded our post and with their superior numbers made a wide gap in our defences. As it was they didn't make another push for several hours. We kept firing on through the night until about half-past five when the tanks appeared. Then we sat tight and watched them go by, as we had been told not to attract attention by firing on them. But it wasn't a very encouraging sight. We had no communication with our other posts and we didn't know if we had been overrun. But we'd been told to stick there and we did.

About forty tanks went through and then we came up and engaged the German infantry and gunners who were trying to bring their guns through the gap. These were easy meat. We shot up their crews before they could get into action, and every time the infantry tried to get through the gap we drove them back with Bren guns and rifles. After the tanks went through no guns and no infantry got past us. Meantime, the British gunners behind us had broken the tank attack, and soon enemy tanks and infantry were scrambling back through the gap. Into this traffic jam we fired everything we had and the Jerries got their worst hiding they'd had up to that time.

One of the British gunners – an anonymous sergeant-major in a 25-pounder battery – provided this account of the German tank attack:

On Easter Monday we got our chance as anti-tank gunners. About forty German tanks broke through the outer perimeter defences and headed for our gun positions about three miles inside. In the half-light of dawn we first engaged them with high-explosive at about 2000 yards. But they came on firing their 75mm guns and machine-guns. With their tracer bullets firing everywhere it looked like Blackpool illuminations.

When they'd got within about 700 yards of us we let them have it over open sights. In a twenty-minute battle our troop fired about 100 rounds per gun, and that stopped them. We knocked out seven with our 25-pounders before they turned back. There was one sticky moment when two heavy tanks tried to get round our flank. The gun I was on hit one tank and it broke down as it tried to struggle back. The other tank hit us, knocking out the gun and most of the crew, but before that our fire had given it such a fright that it withdrew too. That day was the biggest tank and artillery battle in the defence of Tobruk: thirty-eight tanks got inside but seventeen were knocked out by our 25-pounders, anti-tank guns and tanks.

The German failure to overwhelm Tobruk swiftly was an immense irritation to Rommel but he accepted that he must wear down the defenders with repeated aerial and artillery bombardments. For the defenders the German bomber raids became the most constant of the many unpleasant features of life in the fortress. This was a period of German aerial ascendancy as the RAF's resources were limited by other commitments and the distance of its airfields from Tobruk. Stuka raids

A 25-pounder of the Royal Horse Artillery engages Axis targets along the Tobruk perimeter. Although designed as a conventional field artillery piece, the 25-pounder was regularly used in an anti-tank role. (F.2887)

were particularly disliked by the ground troops. L. E. Tutt describes the feeling of being under dive-bomb attack:

A less welcome break in the routine was the occasional Stuka raid on the position. They were stub-winged, almost ungainly in appearance. They looked rather slow-moving in flight until they went into their dive. They came down like a stone, holding their course until it appeared that they were going to dash themselves to pieces on their target, then they would pull out of it with such suddenness that you felt their wings would be torn away.

Under attack, one seemed to have been chosen as their sole target. You could see the bombs leave their racks, wobble hesitantly then straighten up as they gained velocity. We were encouraged to fire at them with our rifles; I think this was solely to help us with our morale. I saw a Stuka that had been brought down by a Bofors team and the area around the pilot was as armoured as a light tank. No rifle bullet could have penetrated it. I once saw an officer solemnly engaging some Italian bombers with his service revolver; they were at least 20,000 feet high.

Jack Daniel was a gunner in 153 Battery, 51st Regiment of Heavy Anti-Aircraft Artillery and despite being a prime target for German dive-bombers he gained a considerable respect for the men trying to kill him:

You had to hand it to them. To get into an aircraft and nose it down through a barrage, which could blast you to smithereens any minute, and dive through it and let go of the bomb and then race back for home with everything in the harbour going at you. Everyone would be firing, 303s, revolvers, anything. We could almost chuck bricks at them as they came whizzing by.

Opposite: A large force of German Ju-87 Stuka dive-bombers flies out to attack British positions. The Stuka was a vital element in the Afrika Korps's armoury, acting as long-range precision artillery. (MH.5591)

British gunners at Tobruk prepare to fire a captured Italian 20mm Breda anti-aircraft gun. The Breda was an effective light anti-aircraft weapon with a ceiling of 8000 feet and a cyclic rate of fire of 200–220 r.p.m. (E.2878)

German aircraft losses mounted steadily and gradually their pilots' enthusiasm began to wane. John Kelly, another AA gunner, noted in his diary for 22 August:

Two Stuka raids today. The first started just before noon. In this raid the planes went out to sea and turned back outside the perimeter on the Bardia Road side. The second lot received a terrific barrage before they got anywhere near the town. We picked them up just south of us and set the ball rolling. The other guns started as they came within range and we finished up with the best 'harbour barrage' I have seen for a long while.

Many of the Stukas dropped their bombs in the sea. They went the same way as those of this morning but one of them turned in too quickly. He came heading for the site and we put up a shot in front of his nose which must have shaken him for he turned off very sharply and headed for his own lines as fast as he could.

Along the perimeter the Australians carried out the aggressive patrolling policy their fathers had established in the First World War; that No Man's Land would be an Australian preserve was an unstated dictum throughout the siege. Despite being a British tankman, H. L. 'Bob' Sykes was posted on his arrival in Tobruk as a reinforcement to an Australian infantry unit. A few days after settling in with the Australians, Sykes had his first taste of combat:

I remember one night I was particularly tired, when just before first light someone stuck his head in my little dump and said, 'Are you there, Bob? You'd better come out with us, some Jerry tanks have broken through.' I staggered out to our Morris truck while in the darkness figures were loading up: petrol bombs, grenades, guns, ammo, the lot. After travelling a long way we came to a barbed-wire barricade – a section was slid apart and we went through. In the distance a small war was going on.

Tanks were moving away from us and we went after one that seemed to be behind. It was a German tank and some of the Aussies raced off behind it and jammed steel rods between the tracks. Petrol bombs lit up the tank; grenades and shots rang out. We swung the truck close to the tank, which was well alight, and the raiding crowd jumped aboard. We had very minor casualties but tension remained very high. We made off along the wire to where the main battle had taken place; one of our Matildas was knocked out with all the crew dead but it looked as if they had made short measure of the eight German tanks that tried to break through.

A field section of the Australian Military History Section was present during the siege of Tobruk. Compiled from various sources is this account of the formation of the Australian Bush artillery:

No better example of the Tobruk garrison's disregard for convention and readiness to meet any contingency could be provided by the Bush artillery – odd batteries of captured Italian field pieces, mostly 75mm and 79mm calibre, manned by engineers and infantry, and used with great effect by these amateur gunners for the purpose of harassing the enemy.

Lacking sights, the guns were aligned by looking along the barrel. Judgement by trial and error was established and a telegraph pole served as an OP. In less

The Bush artillery in action, firing a captured Italian 75mm field gun, 13 August 1941. The gun crews were made up of infantrymen, signallers, orderlies, cooks and any other spare personnel. (E.4788)

than a month the Bush artillery accounted for at least twenty-five enemy MT [motor transport]. Several times it silenced enemy MG fire and assisted fighting patrols returning to the lines. Regular artillery units became interested in its work and sent along Warrant Officers to assist in maintenance.

The Australians were an implacable foe. Bob Braithwaite remembers an incident following the repulse of a German attack:

One poor Jerry was trapped on the wire; wounded, bent double, making a hell of a noise. There was one Aussie, dancing around him with his rifle and bayonet, shouting to his cobbers: 'What shall I do with the bastard?' Silence from the trenches, then a quiet call: 'Stick it up his arse and shut up and get back here, you flaming galah.' This was done.

Despite their robust attitude to the conduct of operations, the Australians were forced to make an accommodation to the climate and the conditions along the perimeter. This led to a degree of mutual co-operation between defenders and attackers. As dusk fell an unofficial armistice was generally observed, to allow the men to bring up food, water and ammunition, while the raising of a Red Cross flag led to a temporary cessation of fire at that point. Out in his observation post (OP) L. E. Tutt was able to watch this phenomenon:

I was in a small, forward weapon pit with one of the Australians who was going through the first-light task of seeing if anything had gone on in the enemy held area in the night. Quite unexpectedly, one of the enemy climbed above ground, moved a few steps away from his trench and started to urinate. I waited for the Australians to open fire on him but, suddenly, there was a great laugh from someone on our side, then two or three of them climbed out and began to do the same.

It was contagious. In a few minutes there must have been about fifty men, friend and foe alike, relieving themselves, shaking out their blankets, trying to toss cigarettes across the intervening space, and generally enjoying a holiday from hate. This must have gone on for about six or seven minutes before the whine of a shell sent everyone diving below ground again and the war was resumed.

As the siege dragged on so the men did what they could to make themselves comfortable, and despite the many shortages ingenious attempts were made to bring a homely touch to otherwise rather grim surroundings. An indefatigable chronicler of the siege, Tutt gives his account of life behind the front line in Tobruk:

The battery commander recognized the therapeutic value of keeping us busy and, once we had done everything that we could to make the command post area safe, allowed us to work for our comfort. My hole in the ground was about seven feet long, four feet wide and five feet deep. In bed at night it felt rather like a cosy coffin. Bed sounds a bit pretentious but it had become *de rigueur* for other ranks to have a bed made of a pole framework with a couple of ground sheets laced across them and resting on four petrol cans.

The ground was a cheesy kind of sandstone in this area and was easily carved out with a jackknife. All along the wall at the side of my bed I had carved out shaped holes to take my personal possessions: mess tins, mug, book and reading lamp, a tobacco tin filled with paraffin and a piece of frayed cord for a wick. It was just enough to read by when I had pulled the old piece of tarpaulin over the hole to keep out the cold and shield my light.

Because of our isolation from all normal sources of supply quite simple things took on a value far beyond their worth. Tinned milk for a private brew, needles for running repairs, razors, tea and tobacco were always sought after. We rolled our own, using any paper we could scrounge. Fortunately the Australians were always more generously endowed. Seldom did I do an OP duty with them and not come away with some cigarette papers and tins of tobacco.

My main deprivation was books of any kind. Having parted from my family some years before I had no one I could appeal to to send me reading material. I had always been an avid reader and the printed word was like a drug to me. I begged them from all and sundry, some of them with wads of pages torn out for cigarette paper so that I had to use my imagination to fill the gaps. Because I was dependent on the reading interests of others my taste became a catholic one. I read *No Orchids for Miss Blandish* followed by *War and Peace. Das Kapital* was a strange companion for *The Pickwick Papers.* I still have by me the three utility, war-time printed Penguins by Adrian Bell: *Corduroy, The Cherry Tree* and *Silver Ley*, a gentle trilogy about the East Anglian countryside which I read in Tobruk and carried in my side pack all through Burma. One glorious find was an omnibus edition of John Buchan's novels. That kept me going for a whole fortnight.

A canteen service was established by the Australian authorities in Tobruk as a means of augmenting the basic rations provided for the troops, although this was always dependent on shipping space. Lieutenant J. Dewhurst describes the activities of the service which he commanded:

Fair stocks of canteen goods were held at Tobruk in April but they were rapidly depleted. After a lean period in May, when ammunition, petrol and rations had priority, shipments started to come through. By the middle of August the number of different items had increased, of which fine-cut tobacco and cigarette papers, chocolate and lime juice were the most popular amongst the troops. Known as 'champagne' to the garrison, lime juice was in particular demand to break down the taste of the brackish and chlorinated water.

With the improvement in the shipping position, the supply of canteen goods became satisfactory, but there was a demand that could never be met – the cry of Tobruk's parched throats for beer. A certain amount of whisky and gin was brought in but rarely enough space could be found for beer.

Major R. B. T. Daniell, a regular artillery officer who had been appointed as second-in-command to the South Notts Hussars, a yeomanry regiment equipped with 25-pounders.

Supplied by fast-running destroyers from Alexandria the lifeline to Tobruk was always kept open. Officers who knew the ropes could use the system to their advantage – as R. B. T. Daniell of the South Notts Hussars demonstrated:

The Navy, of course, was a godsend to us. On the four dark nights of the month, they ran the gauntlet from Alexandria bringing letters, ammunition and a few reinforcements. The destroyer only stayed in the harbour for twenty minutes – on one side the wounded were slung aboard, whilst on the other, boxes of all sorts were sent down a shute into small boats. I was lucky. I had met several of their commanders in Alexandria. They invariably brought with them a sealed two-gallon tin, filled with welcome whisky, food and clean clothes, carefully packed by my wife and clearly marked 'Nails of all sizes' to delude the wandering Australians. I only lost one to a looter. I then repaired to the wardroom and downed all the whisky I could hold before dejectedly throwing myself down the shute.

The constant round of aerial and artillery bombardment, coupled with a poor diet and relentless hard work began to take its toll on the garrison. Even as early as the end of May, Kelly noted in his diary: 'We have had a pretty rough time. Most of the fellows are worn out and skin diseases are prevalent. Living in the desert is no picnic. Several chaps have been sent to base because their nerves were broken.' As the summer wore on even the normally cheerful Bob Sykes was forced to concede:

We have no pleasures, not in a besieged town. Never did I see anyone cracking up under the strain but there were quite a lot of them 'desert happy' or part crazy. As to be expected, the boozing had dropped down to a very low level, only an occasional bottle of beer came in, and a very small quantity of rum.

I had an awful feeling of the loss of time: one day was much as another, we had difficulty finding the date. At one time I was really worried I could not remember the month, and for that matter neither could most of the others.

We knew nothing of the war outside; some tried to make up radios but we got more rumours than truth. The population in this besieged harbour town never got any less. The cemetery grew in size and more reinforcements were ferried in. Life here was more than tough: the heat by day, the cold by night and the continuous air raids and shelling made one feel it was going on for ever, and that we were actually living in an earthly Hell.

N. C. Rogers had been sent to Tobruk in the latter stages of the siege as medical officer for the 4th Royal Tank Regiment. He reported on the state of the men's health:

There was a lot of jaundice about. In those days we called it catarrhal jaundice; hepatitis it's called these days. Jaundice is a very depressing sort of illness. People get very, well, very jaundiced in their outlook. And this was quite striking among a lot of the Aussies we met, that they were either getting or recovering from jaundice.

One aspect of the siege – and indeed of the war as a whole – which particularly irritated the men was the official statements issued on their behalf. While threatening pronouncements from the likes of Lord Haw-Haw were greeted with ribald amusement, tub-thumping jingoism from one's own side was another matter. Kelly's entry for 14 August succinctly captures the mood of men fed up with official bull:

JERRY COMMUNIQUÉ: 'The men of Tobruk are tired and worn out and we shall keep them besieged until the end of the war.'
OUR COMMUNIQUÉ: 'The men of Tobruk are in fine fettle and are waiting for the word "Go!" All the men in Tobruk have had a month's leave.'
MY COMMUNIQUÉ: 'Dr Goebbels has been out-lied at last.'

Yet for all the privations suffered by the troops, strong bonds of comradeship developed that helped transcend everyday discomforts and fears. As in the trenches of the Great War, the sense of community of men in adverse circumstances was an experience of extraordinary power, and was remembered long after the siege. Tutt looks back at the period with a degree of real fondness:

I found that life in Tobruk in some strange way satisfied a need that I had within me. Prior to the war I had run away from home and lived in an attic room in Camden Town. It had been a lonely existence. My present situation offered companionship and the satisfaction of being an essential, if very minor, part of a larger society. I now found myself with friends.

Of course I was aware of the danger in our situation and I no more wanted to die than anyone else. Yet no one beyond the perimeter was seeking to kill me personally. It might happen by accident but it wouldn't be a matter of dislike for me as an individual. There were the raids, the dust, the dysentery, the hunger, the thirst, the desert sores; all very unpleasant, but not more than one could take with companions equally afflicted. No one woke up to a new day with the feeling that it was more than we could face. I do not think that my morale was any better than any other man's. It was good everywhere.

Not one man who took part in the siege can have remained unchanged by it. Very few men outside the small select band who played a part in the life of Tobruk can ever have experienced the same unity of feeling and purpose.

Polish troops take up a firing position on the Tobruk perimeter. Although an obviously contrived photograph, it effectively conveys the aggressive attitude of the Poles towards the Germans. (E.6046)

There was a 'oneness' about our daily existence. When I heard a burst of firing coming from one of the posts on our front I could see in my mind's eye the tall Australian with his battered bush hat, a finger on the trigger of his Bren. I could almost hear what he was saying to his Number Two: 'Come on Bluey, let's give the buggers a couple of magazines full – let 'em know we're still here.'

Bob Sykes agreed with Tutt on the human factor in the siege: 'The comradeship that sprung up between us has left such a deep memory. I have never known anything like it nor ever will.' Jack Daniel: 'This companionship was about all we had when you come to think about it. Whether a chap shared his cigarettes or whatever he mucked in – that was vital really. You got to know each other terribly well.'

During August the British government had received requests from the Australian government for the withdrawal of its troops from Tobruk. Despite the problems of an amphibious withdrawal from a town under siege, the Royal Navy began the operation and by the end of September most of the Australians had been replaced by a mixed group of British and Polish troops, along with a Czech and later two New Zealand battalions. Amongst the old hands, Tutt recorded the departures and arrivals:

Gradually we rubbed the names of Australian units off the talc on our map boards and replaced them with British ones. The gen was that the Poles were coming. We wondered what kettle of fish they would be. The Poles proved to be the legendary Carpathian Brigade, fearsome soldiers with a great singleness of purpose. They didn't mind how far they went, or how difficult it was to get there, as long as their destination offered them the chance to kill Germans. After the war I was to become friendly with a Polish artist who had served with them in Tobruk. He told me that when they were told that they were coming up to relieve the Australians the whole unit broke into cheers.

They moved into our old sector, Pilastrino, and they soon started a very aggressive policy with regard to the troops occupying the salient. We learned to look out for them when we went to ration or water point. '*Dzien Dobry*,' we greeted them and they returned our salutation with a slight bow and a click of the heels. All a bit different from the Aussies, who normally returned our well wishes with an affectionate 'Get stuffed!'

The reinforcement of Tobruk was not just carried out to replace the Australians but also to provide a springboard force which would link up with a new British advance into Libya – Operation Crusader (*see* Part Two, page 54). The breakout was set for the night of 21/22 November but it would not be until 10 December that the siege was finally broken. For the men on the ground it was not so much a moment for wild rejoicing as simply a relief from the bombing and shelling. There were some compensations, however, as Jack Daniel explained:

There was just a tremendous lull in the fighting as the Jerries withdrew to Benghazi; nothing in the air, no machine-guns, no mortars thumping away up over the hill. Gradually it was the quiet that told us that Tobruk was relieved, for the moment anyway. Then it became official that we were to be relieved and I think the final seal came when we were all told to go to a certain map reference away from the guns – much to our mystification. And there in the desert, still within the perimeter, was this huge pile of crates. We were all told this was a present from Mr Watney: it was beer unlimited. It was all free and we were given two days to do what we liked. The scenes were quite unbelievable. We all got totally stupefied. I can remember crawling about on all fours. I didn't know if it was night or day, nor did anyone else. It was a marvellous gesture. We knew it was over then.

Life in the Desert

After a short period getting used to local conditions in one of the encampments around Port Tewfik or Ismailia, the British soldier would begin his march to the front line. The length of the journey depended on the current state of success of the British armed forces: the longer the distance, the greater the British success.

To the vast majority of men the desert came as shock. Not only were the physical conditions particularly enervating – the extremes of heat and cold, the shortage of water and the vast distances to be covered – but the empty landscape that stretched to the horizon imposed its own psychological strain. Despite this, each soldier had to come to terms with his new environment, and for all but a few, acclimatization took place over time.

The desert was not the sandy, seaside beach on a large scale that so many soldiers imagined. Rough, rocky ground alternated with patches of soft sand and gravel, while almost sheer cliffs rose up from the coastal littoral to the broad upland plateaux of the desert proper. The terrain grew more varied as the soldier ventured southward from the coast. James Patch, a gunner in the Royal Artillery, answered a call for volunteers to join the Long Range Desert Group (*see* Private Armies, page 189) and gave this account of driving over the desert:

There were all kinds of different surfaces to travel on. There was the seria, for instance: mile after mile of perfectly smooth hard sand. I've seen a truck going along at 60 mph across the seria with nobody in the driving cab at all. The driver would set his hand throttle and the truck would just go on. And we knew we weren't going to hit any bumps or obstacles. All four members of the crew would get on the back of the truck and just let it go.

At other times, though, just getting through soft sand was another matter altogether. We often had to dig our way with sand trays all day long – and that was quite exhausting. At other times you'd have to zigzag all day through rocks and up and down wadis.

In the desert, accurate navigation was essential. On some occasions this could literally be a matter of life and death, although at others it took on a more comical aspect. An officer in the Intelligence Corps, R. H. Dahl, had been despatched from his HQ to interrogate a German prisoner captured in the Crusader battles. After a fruitless encounter Dahl made ready to get back to base:

I set out to return by compass bearing to our ACV [Armoured Command Vehicle] with HQ, XXX Corps. But with light failing my driver and I got hopelessly lost and I decided to sit and sleep it out until daybreak in our hard,

Sappers from a South African
Field Survey Company map
out a position deep in the
Western Desert. Accurate
maps were not only essential
for navigation but also for
precisely noting the positions
of the minefields dotted
across Egypt and Libya.
(E.12777)

cold scout car. At first light we set off over the crest of a nearby slope and there, before our eyes, were all our HQ vehicles which had been hidden by the rising ground. Success had eluded us in the previous evening by a quarter mile.

Richard Bromley-Gardner was a captain in the 2nd Highland Light Infantry when his battalion was sent up into the desert in March 1942 as part of the 5th Indian Division:

The first time one goes up into the desert one is completely amazed by the flat terrain. We used to motor around the desert finding our way by sun compass. It was a gadget which had been produced by British officers in the 1930s [in fact, by Ralph Bagnold of the LRDG – *see* Private Armies, page 189]. It was a very accurate compass. Roughly, the sun marked the nomen – the same piece of equipment you have on a sundial clock – which threw a shadow, and if your compass was correctly set, that was the mark you kept your direction on.

At various places across the desert there would be a cairn or a barrel, a known spot that would be numbered. If it was a barrel it would have on it a figure like 123 in great white letters. That would be known as barrel 123 and would be one of the marks that you would use when trying to navigate through the desert.

The Field Survey Companies were responsible for erecting these guides to navigation. An established artist in civilian life, Colin Hayes had joined up after Dunkirk and his talents were used in surveying and map making:

The job was to put up beacons at intervals of about 10 miles square, made up of forty-gallon petrol drums with numbers on the base, and then accurately position them on the map. They had to be set up and surveyed, mostly from astronomical observations; as no survey had been done before there were no fixed points. The information was then rushed back to the printing section and overprinted on every fresh batch of maps. So a map would consist of a grid and lots of numbers and dots. Occasionally it would have something like 'many tracks' written on it as well, just to make it look as if there was something else there. But mostly it was more like a naval chart than a map.

The 8th Durham Light Infantry was one of the battalions of the 50th Infantry Division. Harold Sell, an officer in the battalion, describes some of the problems encountered in desert driving:

If you're moving in a large formation across the desert it's not easy, so you'd have navigating officers using the sun compass. But the average driver had to improvise. They would put a string from the bonnet of the vehicle up to a row of nails on top of the cab and every hour they switched the string one notch along. The driver simply drove along the shadow on top of the bonnet and that kept him in the right direction.

You had to stop every hour to check your tyres and let some air out or else they burst with the heat. Then you had to check to see the sand hadn't got into the carburettors. All this maintenance went on every hour as you drove. At the same time you adjusted your compasses and checked your weapons. It was a drill which was carried out without any bother. You checked your petrol, you checked your oil, you checked your water.

Along with the flies the most irksome feature of life in the desert was the sandstorm. Bob Sykes vividly recalls his first experience during his attachment to an Australian unit in the defence of Tobruk:

I was cleaning my rifle and .38 [revolver] when one of the Aussies said: 'I should wrap them up well, Bob, we're in for a Quennie of a dust storm.' I could not see anything, and I couldn't see how he could tell. But after about an hour I heard a very new noise, rather like a train coming, and way out a big black bank of cloud was rushing towards us. The Aussie said: 'Get your clobber inside, put your blanket over the entrance and get in quick.'

I thought I had seen it all up to now but this was a new one on me. The sandstorm came at us like an express train at about 40 mph with increasing gusts of wind. All the oxygen seemed to go out of the air, and the flies were maddening and swarming. The heat was terrific and I sweated so the sand caked onto me – in my eyes, nose and ears. I sat down in my dugout and waited, thinking it would be over in a few minutes, but suddenly I nearly panicked – the sand was coming through every crack. I thought I would be buried. I fought my way out. I could hardly stand up in the wind. The sand was whipping the skin off my face and hands.

It was almost pitch dark and I felt entirely alone. Then a light appeared and the sun began to look like a dirty orange. The noise slowly abated and the wind died down: I had ridden out my first sandstorm. As we brushed the sand off our

Looking like a great dark wall, a sandstorm roars across the desert plain. Sandstorms caused the troops intense discomfort and were one of the few things to bring military operations to a halt. (E.17824)

faces so they bled. One of them I hardly recognized said, 'What a beaut, I told you she'd be a real Quennie.'

For the hardened soldier the sandstorms, the heat and the flies were borne for the most part with a stoic equanimity. For other servicemen, newly flung into the region, it was a more difficult proposition. Flying Officer G. A. Stillingfleet's fighter squadron had been withdrawn from Malta and his new desert billet was not to his liking:

I soon discovered that desert life was no picnic. Drinking distilled seawater which was hot and salty didn't quench our thirst but just kept us alive. There was nothing we could get that would quench our thirst, in fact we had a perpetual thirst that almost drove us crazy. Thirst is a terrible thing, but the imagination is worse: we would lay awake at nights thinking of milkshakes, lemonades, cider and ice-cold water from mountain streams.

In the day time we were nearly driven crazy by the terrific heat and the thousands of flies. At nights the lice, bugs and cockroaches tormented us and the sandstorms arose covering our mouths, noses and hair with fine sand. Sometimes they got so bad it was considered unwise to venture from your tent. One night a friend of mine went to see a friend of his in a tent a hundred yards away. He missed it and was lost for fourteen hours.

The desert produced its own special monotony, exacerbated by sand-storms. H. A. Wilson arrived in Egypt in March 1941 as a clerk in a Royal Engineer water-boring section. His diary for September illus-trated the tedium of life in the 'Blue':

FRIDAY 19: Tummy trouble. Hot weather – sandstorm.
SATURDAY 20: OC went on leave to Palestine. More dust.
WEDNESDAY 24: Weary of the desert and sick of it all.
THURSDAY 25: Nothing to delight in these days – tired of the desert.
FRIDAY 26: Today was absolutely dreadful. Dust, dust, dust, blowing all the time, every second, every minute, every hour for sixteen hours. It blew in through the office door, poured down through the skylight, covered books, papers, files, ink bottles and typewriter. Poor old typewriter! It's clogged but it still keeps turning out the letters.

Dust! Every breath I took sucked it down my throat and into the pit of my stomach. It blew into our mess-tins and settled on every bite we ate. Our clothes and blankets were thick with it. Why the hell did I ever join up!

Tempers were on edge all day – I didn't meet one good-natured person. In the evening the men quarrelled in the new canteen, and came to blows. Can't say I blame them – this desert is enough to drive a man mad, myself included; but I have a diary to get mad in.
SATURDAY 27: Today was clear and tranquil, and everyone was back in good humour again, as if man and nature had agreed to make amends for yester-day's contretemps.

Another, more bizarre, consequence of sandstorms was related by Louis Challoner, a gunner in the 2nd Regiment RHA: 'The flying dust also charged the metal parts of vehicles with electricity. Shorts became frequent and stopped some vehicles altogether, while from others,

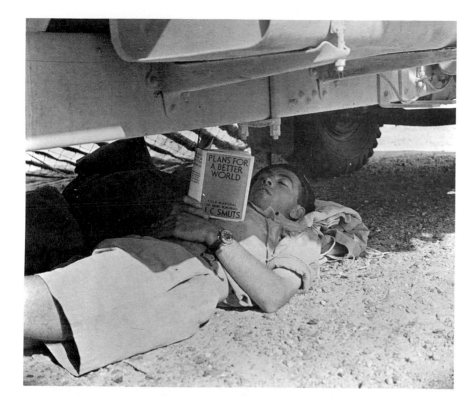

A soldier of the HQ squadron of 2nd Armoured Brigade looks forward to a better world. Books were always in short supply in the desert and many private initiatives were undertaken to secure a supply of reading matter. In this unit £25 was collected and 120 books bought for a squadron lending library. A percentage breakdown of the troops' preferences revealed the following results: thrillers and Westerns 30%; essays, biographies and 'literary' novels 30%; short stories 10%; poetry and plays 5%; humour 10%; war books 15%.

personnel got unaccountable electric shocks which were mildly disconcerting.'

Whereas sandstorms were relatively short-lived if violent, flies were a perpetual irritation. Harold Sell complained: 'There were thousands of flies. They were hardbacked green things, very large, like the big black fly that we have at home. They'd be in your eyes, your ears, everything, and you couldn't do anything about it.' J. G. Harris, an NCO in the 7th Rifle Brigade, illustrated a common problem:

Flies were a terrible nuisance. More often than not you'd be drinking a cup of tea and you would have to put your hand over the top and sip it between the thumb and finger to stop the flies, otherwise they would be lining up around the rim to dive in.

Water and its conservation was of prime importance in a region that had limited sources of supply. Apart from a few wells and desalination plants in the major ports, water had to be laboriously transported up to the front line in tanker lorries. In the desert each man was issued with a daily water ration, ranging from four to six pints, half of it going to the cookhouse for the communal preparation of food, the remainder issued directly as a water-bottle ration.

Like so many things in the desert, experience was all; careful conservation would ensure that each man would have enough to drink with a little left over for washing purposes. By the summer of 1942 Harold Sell had become an old hand:

Everybody had a tin like a petrol can in which he kept his water for washing in.

One of the methods used by troops in the desert to recycle water. Dirty water is poured into an improvised filtering system made out of four-gallon petrol cans; the filter element is provided by a layer of sand and small stones in the top can. (E.12285)

We used captured Italian gas masks, took the filters off them – which were very good – and put them in the top of the tins. When you had your water-bottle ration – and you had to be very meagre with it – you cleaned your teeth, swilled your mouth out and spat it into the filter to run back into the can. When you had built up half a can of water you washed your face in it, then back into filter again. Then you might wash your socks in it and then put it into the can and back. So you had a perpetual motion of water recycling; the water in your can might be weeks old.

J. G. Harris described the progressive stages which a given quantity of water might go through:

In the morning you cleaned your teeth and spat out the tiny bit of water you had in your mouth. Then you gave yourself a shave in it before putting it into the radiator of the truck. After about three miles the driver and his passenger would be smelling like lavender because the old shaving foam used to come off the radiator and blow into the truck. Never a drop of water wasted.

Troops stationed on the coast sometimes attempted to distill sea water. A. H. McGee found this a far from easy task:

I remember on one occasion I spent twelve hours just getting six gallons of sea water for tea that evening. We made up a distillery with a couple of forty-gallon drums and some old copper tubing. I collected driftwood which had washed in from the sea and boiled the water, the steam going up through a copper pipe and dripping into another water tank.

Using water to wash clothes in the desert was generally considered too wasteful of resources and other methods were adopted. Harold Fitz-john: 'At times we managed to scrounge some petrol and take our shirts and shorts off, throw them in the petrol and then onto the sand. In ten minutes we could put them back on again – perfectly laundered with no smell.'

For the men in the front line there was a natural resentment towards those back at base who were not enduring the privations and dangers of the desert. Harold Sell recalls an example of this attitude:

We imagined that every staff officer who was in Cairo lived in the lap of luxury, that was to say he had water. I remember on one of the circulars that came round, a wag who had written a long poem about these staff officers in Cairo who he called the 'Gaberdine Swine' – as their uniforms were made from gaberdine material. At the end of every stanza he had put in a chorus: 'And every time they pulled the chain/ Went three days' rations down the drain'.

To make matters worse, the quality of the water was often very poor. L. E. Tutt noted: 'We rarely drank water as such; it was foul stuff to drink in its natural form. It was much more satisfying to have as a brew.' There were still problems, however: 'It often curdled the tinned milk that we used in our tea so that the mugs became filled with soft, orange-coloured curds'. Despite this, 'we could never get enough tea, sugar and tinned milk. Our mugs of scalding sweet tea became a drug and to be deprived of them was sheer hell. Morale and good fellowship were directly proportional to our supply of brews.'

Tea was recognized by all to be an essential part of the British soldier's equipment. John Longstaff was merely holding a widely acknowledged opinion when he said: 'In my view a cup of char won the war. Give a Tommy a cup of char and whatever morale he had before-hand it was right high up after his cuppa char.' The higher authorities were as aware of the importance of tea as the regimental quartermaster: in 1942 the British government undertook to buy up the world's yearly crop, distributing the surplus to other Allied nations. The soldiers' need for a brew was all the greater as there was next to nothing else to drink in the desert; the appearance of alcohol was infrequent and, anyway, lacked the refreshing qualities of tea.

Food was for the most part plentiful but desert conditions ensured that it was fairly unpalatable, despite the best efforts of the cooks. Ad hoc cooking arrangements were the norm when troops were on the

A petrol can cooker. The bottom end of another can is used as the frying pan to cook rashers of bacon. (E.20360)

Men in an anti-aircraft emplacement treat themselves to a rare feast to celebrate Christmas 1942. The photograph was taken a little prematurely, on 17 December, to allow time for the picture to get back to Britain by Christmas (E.20242)

move. D. A. Main was a soldier in the 7th Rifle Brigade. After a few weeks in the 'Blue' – the troops' term for the desert – he considered he and his men had gained a basic proficiency in desert matters. On the preparation of food he wrote:

Some of the riflemen had made a cooker by welding a large biscuit tin. A small cheese tin was cut in two, and into one half was put some sand and petrol to be used as fuel. The welded biscuit tin had a funnel through the middle, surrounded by a water jacket which contained a gallon of water which could be brought to the boil within three minutes.

When we were on the move one rifleman sat in the back of the truck with a hammer, with which he hit the hard biscuits contained in a sandbag until they were crumbled and could be used as an substitute for porridge – to which was added condensed milk, jam, sugar and hot water.

In more fixed circumstances, the cookhouse achieved a greater prominence. The results were usually less than appetizing, however. L. E. Tutt:

Once a whistle had been blown to tell us that we could 'stand down' it was straight to the hole where Charley Blowers was sweating over our breakfast. The mug of tea gradually changed us into something resembling human beings, as its warmth drove away the hollow gutted ache in our insides. I tended to eat little at breakfast. It was usually nothing more promising than half a ladle of biscuit burgoo, army biscuits soaked overnight in water to a mush and sweetened with sugar and laced with a little tinned milk. I never came to terms with the occasional change to Canadian tinned bacon: a few slivers of pink in a solid tin of lardy fat.

The main meal of the day came with dusk but again the cooks were forced to use a very limited range of ingredients:

Bully beef, tinned M and V [meat and vegetables], dehydrated potatoes, herrings in tomato and any odds and ends of Italian rations the Quartermaster had sent him. With the best will in the world this meant some kind of stew for nine meals out of ten. The cooks tried their best to ring the changes but it was very difficult.

Bully beef fritters were a popular meal until the MO banned them because of the high fat content. Occasionally a couple of tablespoonfuls of curry were thrown into the stew for a bit of variety. An attempt to provide some green vegetables by giving us dehydrated cabbage was a hundred per cent failure. No matter how the cook prepared it, it always ended up looking and tasting like stewed gas cape. There was always a crate of army biscuits at hand from which you could take as many as you wanted and, best of all, a full mug of tea.

Despite the openness and size of the desert, troops were gathered together in tightly packed groups, which inevitably led to the problem of waste disposal. Armies had much experience in this and the provision of latrines was well established. Desert conditions merely brought forth special solutions. Harold Sell recounts the system encountered in the Gazala boxes:

Latrine provision had to vary according to what sort of soil you were on. If some part of the area was relatively soft you could dig down latrines. Otherwise you had to use thunder boxes and carry them to these places. But the drill was always the same: every morning the sanitary squad would go round with tins of petrol, pour it into the latrine and light it to burn everything up. And then you had what they called the 'desert rose' – the urinals. They used to put one tin on top of another, and clip them together with another big tin on the top, stuck into the sand.

The monotony of desert life was occasionally relieved by home-grown diversions. Scorpions were a dangerous nuisance but they provided a degree of sport for the troops. Scorpion fights were a common occurrence, as A. H. McGee recounts:

We used to dig out a ring of sand and put in a drop of petrol, light it and put a couple of scorpions in the centre. They'd fight it out – there's nothing like the sting of a scorpion's tail – and if a scorpion got in a tight corner his tail used to come over and kill himself.

While one soldier cleans his rifle another prepares to butcher a freshly shot gazelle – an occasional supplement to standard rations. (E.12400)

Blood sports on a larger scale consisted of gazelle hunts, which had the added bonus of supplementing the rations. The hunters would chase the gazelles in trucks and blaze away at them with their rifles. H. A. Wilson joined one such party:

We spied six of them in a line. The distance was only about five hundred yards. All of us fired at once, hitting three. One went down on the spot, another kept limping on and the third kept falling and rising alternately. When we arrived we found the fallen gazelle still alive but unable to get up as his leg had been blown off. Nevertheless he made frantic, pathetic efforts to do so. As I watched him I was struck with pity for the little animal. But the fact that we were in need of meat put salve on my conscience.

I shall never forget the death of that animal. At first we decided to blow its brains out at close range but somebody said it would make too much of a mess that way, so Skinner elected to stand ten yards away and put a bullet through the brains. Skinner fired, the head was hit, thick blood spouted from the hole but the gazelle didn't die. It began to jerk and quiver spasmodically.

Tomes came next, and his shot grazed the ears of the twitching gazelle, whose terror-stricken eyes stared at us, soft, brown and lovable. 'Here lend me a rifle,' Harris demanded in the tone of one who has perfect faith in his marksmanship. Incredible as it seems, he missed. The gazelle wasn't dead yet and there was another dying and in pain twenty yards away.

My turn came next and I discovered my magazine was empty. With an exclamation of exasperation Skinner took his gun and, making sure there was a bullet up the spout, stood over the unfortunate animal and put a bullet through its head. But again this must have missed the brain for it still lived and twitched. Once again Skinner fired from the same position and this shot was definitely the *coup de grace*: the gazelle's head rose in a spasmodic jerk, the whole frame quivered for a fleeting moment, and then the head and three outstretched legs descended to the sands in the stiffness of death.

The other gazelle was in a mess, for this animal had a big hole in its side out of which intestines protruded. It also received its quota of bullets, but the shots were good ones, all into the head. Never again, I vowed, would I hunt a living creature – at any rate unless I had the adequate means to despatch it instantly, without pain and without a scene.

When the gazelles were cut up and cooked many of the 'others didn't fancy it much' although Wilson considered the livers to be 'tender and sweet'.

Gazelles and other larger forms of wildlife were encountered only infrequently by the British soldier. Similarly elusive were contacts with the indigenous people of the desert. When they did happen they almost inevitably involved trade of some sort. According to Harold Fitzjohn, the exchanges were not always completely straightforward:

Although a rare occurrence, some simple barter trade was carried out – British tea for Arab eggs. The nomad would always ask for a written chit or pass to demonstrate his loyalty to the British cause. He'd ask the Germans for the same. I suppose he had a pocket full of them. We used to make one out for him, and it used to say: 'Whatever happens, do not trust the bastard.' After much thanking and 'salaaming' he would go on his way clutching his pass.

Senussi Arabs engage in some friendly barter with a British soldier in Libya. Cigarettes were a standard means of exchange, both in the barrackroom and out in the open desert. (E.21848)

If some men found the desert a tedious and unfriendly place it would seem that many more developed an appreciation for its space and rugged grandeur. A last word can be left to Fitzjohn: 'I liked being in the desert. It was a good healthy life. I can't explain the peace on a night, the sky – how marvellous it was.'

Casualties

Advances made during the Great War and after in the treatment of wounded men ensured that casualties in the Second World War stood an improved chance of survival. Surgical techniques had developed since 1918 – especially with burns – but equally important were the strides made in medical treatment.

In his detailed study of the combat soldier in the Second World War, John Ellis[1] stresses the important of the introduction of penicillin, sulphonamides and blood transfusions. Unfortunately, for many casualties of the Desert War, penicillin and sulpha drugs only came into general use in the latter stages of the North African campaign, but a well-established if basic blood transfusion system was in use in the desert from 1940 onwards – saving men both from loss of blood and from shock, thereby allowing doctors to perform vital, immediate surgery.

The passage of a casualty from the point where he received his wound along the chain of treatment to a general hospital was long and involved. Transportation was a major difficulty. The vast distances over which the armies fought – along with the confusing mobility of military operations – often prevented the swift treatment so essential for traumatic injuries. Only air evacuation would solve this problem – but this would not be fully practicable until the development of the helicopter in the early 1950s.

Each soldier was equipped with a field dressing. If hit, he or a comrade was expected to apply it to the wound to staunch the flow of blood and prevent further infection. The wounded man would attempt to get back to the RAP (Regimental Aid Post). If not he would await the arrival of stretcher-bearers who followed up behind every assault to pick up the seriously wounded.

The RAP was responsible for assessing the injury and, if serious, carrying out emergency surgery before sending the casualty along the chain. Behind the front line were the ADS (Advanced Dressing Station) and MDS (Main Dressing Station) where essential treatment was carried out – blood transfusions, operations to remove shell splinters and the 'tidying-up' of emergency amputations from the RAP. From there the casualty would go to the CCS (Casualty Clearing Station) where full surgery could be performed and then on to a general hospital for recuperation and further treatment where necessary.

Edgar Randolph joined the AIF (Australian Imperial Force) as a nurse in June 1940. Arriving in Egypt in November he soon found

---

[1] *The Sharp End of War* by John Ellis (David & Charles, 1980)

A British medical officer (centre) tends a wounded German prisoner during the opening phase of the Crusader battle, November 1941. (E.6789)

himself caught up in the first offensive against the Italians. Casualties had been light until the assault on Tobruk got under way on 21 January. Then:

The casualties poured in. My mate, Bob Smith, and I were on the go for three days and two nights with no more rest than a ten-minute sit-down. The place was like a butcher's shop. An Aussie DOA (Dead On Arrival) was passed to me to prepare for burial and lack of experience showed in the lad's death. He had a wound in his chest which had been covered with a field dressing. He was then whipped on to a stretcher and carried several miles. I had to get Smithy to help separate him from the stretcher as he had an exit wound in his back that you could put a fist into – not looked for and not treated. The poor devil had bled to death while he was being carried in.

At times medical officers were required to conduct surgery in the most primitive of conditions. It remains a testimony to their skill that so many of their patients survived the rigours of these operations. Captain M. J.

Pleydell, a doctor in the RAMC, had been posted to Egypt and kept up a steady correspondence with his family in Britain. In a letter dated 6 October 1942 Pleydell recounts his adventures after an SAS raid on Benghazi, a good example of the enthusiasm for medical detail and knockabout humour typical of young doctors:

Everything is OK at this end after a fairly busy time. It's funny having to do all the anaesthetics and operating oneself, although occasionally I had an orderly to assist. I started off with a fractured femur, which I had to do with us on the back of a lorry. I had to keep him well under with morphia. Then I had two men wounded after driving over a Thermos bomb – one with extensive second-degree burns over the chest, abdomen, arms and legs, and one who died quietly during the night. I gave the other man with the amputation two pints of plasma, and he lived. Not bad, amputating with an officer to help me and the dust blowing. We had to hurry to catch up with the others, and driving behind in the lorry it was hell to watch three legs and one stump being flung into the air and falling back each time the lorry hit a bump. So we tied

A captured German doctor looks after a British soldier, wounded in the face during Operation Crusader, November/December 1941. The medical services of Germany and Britain upheld the Hippocratic oath. (E.6795)

45

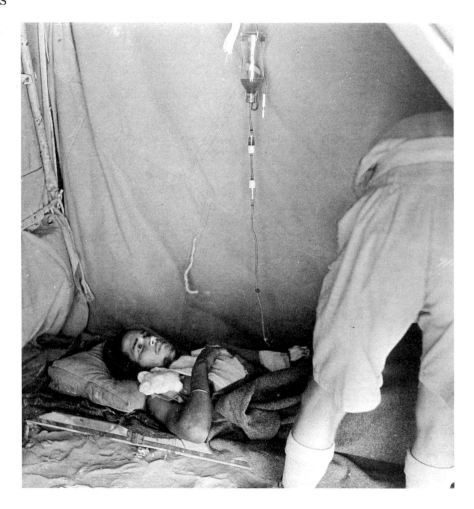

their legs down with a rope. The dust was thrown up and fell all over them, so they became yellow, and we had to stop now and then to bathe their faces and let them breathe.

Later on I had a case of multiple wounds. Not too bad: one shot through the lung, for which there was little to do; one with a compact fracture of the humerus, radius and ulna, with the arm shattered in two places. I left the arm on. All the bad injuries had two pints of blood plasma and I waited until they were stronger before operating.

The last case was a retention of urine due to the perineal urethra being shot away. Unable to find the proximal end of the urethra, eventually I had to do a supra pubic cystotomy. It was the devil. I was wondering if I would open the peritoneum or what. Again I was alone. With nobody retracting and no retractors it's damned difficult to see what you are doing.

When I got back to the others, I found we had no room for stretcher cases as we had lost a good deal of our transport, so I brought back two major wounded and all the minor cases. One was the chap with the shattered arm and the other with multiple wounds. They both made the long trek home OK.

Once an offensive was under way it was essential that medical facilities should keep up with the battle. There were situations where dressing

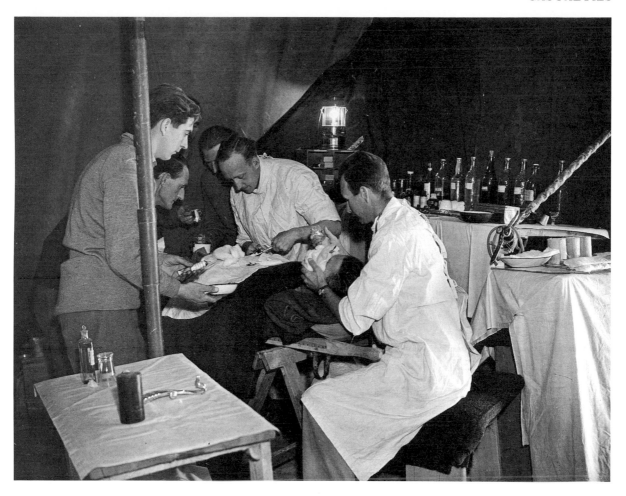

stations found themselves directly in the front line. Major Melzer was in command of an MDS supporting the advance of 5th South African Infantry Brigade during the Crusader battles of November–December 1941. The brigade was virtually wiped out as a fighting entity and casualties were heavy. The fighting was also extremely confused and the MDS was regularly bypassed by German, Italian and British columns as the battle raged around them. Melzer's report on the activities of his MDS noted one potentially disastrous episode:

At about 1300 hours on 23 November the burial of twenty bodies was about to be begin. The medical officers and orderlies were all working at full pressure, and I had just completed a plaster cast. Suddenly, the tank battle started. As no slits had been dug for the casualties who had been coming in all day, we all lay on tarpaulins. I was able to see the entire battle which started on the left of B echelon, the British tanks being about 400 yards to the west of the MDS. As the battle progressed they were gradually pushed back, closer and closer to us. Eventually they reached us, and our tanks actually worked their way between the groups of casualties lying on the ground. By this time the German tanks could be seen on the horizon, the MDS lying between the German and British tanks and the German tanks coming nearer.

Surgery is performed on a wounded soldier in a Main Dressing Station near Bardia, 4 January 1941. (E.1546)

They eventually reached us. My greatest concern was whether they would show the same consideration the British did, and not drive their tanks over the casualties. My fears, however, were quite unfounded because the German tanks kept clear of the persons lying on the ground, and not one of the casualties or personnel was run over by a tank. Soon after, their infantry and recovery vehicles arrived and we were all taken prisoner.

For the next three days Melzer and his MDS worked under Axis control, treating the wounded from all combatant nations. The Germans were particularly impressed with the professional and impartial attitude of the South African doctors and medical staff. Melzer himself noted: 'Many calls for blood donors were made for German and Italian casualties, and Sgt Steyn of this unit gave blood for a German casualty.' Eventually the tide of battle turned against the Axis forces and the MDS was liberated by New Zealand troops.

From the ADS or MDS the wounded were sent down the line to the CCS, which in the Western Desert could mean rail journeys of 200 miles or more. After adventures in Greece and Crete, Dr Theodore Stephanides had been appointed as Orderly Medical Officer at a CCS near the Delta. One of his duties was to meet the casualties off the train and organize their despatch to hospital:

Certainly there was nothing more calculated to strip war of all its false glamour than to wait on a chilly platform and by the feeble rays of electric torches (owing to the blackout) to get scores of stretchers – each containing a poor battered human wreck – off a hospital train. The grim silence made it all the more sinister. Rarely did the wounded utter a moan unless they happened to be delirious. In fact the harder hit they were, the more stoically they generally behaved; it was sometimes the people with little the matter with them who made the most complaint. But even this was rare; the only sounds were an occasional order to the stretcher-bearers and the scrape of ammunition boots on the platform.

A number of orderlies and ambulancemen working in the big Delta hospitals were conscientious objectors. Ronald Joynes had arrived in Egypt with a Quaker ambulance unit after a circuitous journey via Finland and the Soviet Union. He recounts an unusual episode in a ward for wounded Libyan troops (part of the Italian colonial forces):

We saw examples of man's inhumanity to man. Some of the Egyptian orderlies were dreadfully uncaring towards those poor Libyans, even though it was sensible to send them to Egyptian hospitals because they spoke Arabic. There I saw one of the best left hooks ever – delivered by a Quaker from Bristol, to an Egyptian orderly who deliberately picked up a Libyan with a broken arm by his broken arm.

Although it might have been a surprise to an observer of the long hospital trains steaming back from the front to the Delta, battle casualties amounted to only a small proportion of the total demands made on the medical services. Injuries from motor accidents and the movement of heavy machinery were more numerous; the Eighth Army was particularly 'accident prone'. But in the Middle East theatre of operations

Along with other routine maintenance, the crew of a British Crusader
III engages in the task of cleaning out the tank's six-pounder gun.
(TR 939)

A British 5.5-inch gun bombards enemy positions. One of the best medium artillery pieces of the war, the 5.5-inch gun could fire a 100 lb shell to a range in excess of 15,000 yards. (TR 1004)

A Hudson transport
aircraft of the RAF flies
over the pyramids in
Egypt. (TR 26)

A Hurricane of the Desert
Air Force strafes Axis
armour as part of a
ground-attack sortie.
(TR 1012)

Above: British war correspondents and cameramen crane forward to hear a briefing. Despite reservations from some senior officers the reporter had become an integral element of the war machine. (TR 1397)

Left: British troops prepare a Bofors anti-aircraft gun for action. (TR 940)

Above: British soldiers rest beside their Bren carriers during a break in the fighting in the final phase of the war in North Africa. (TR 631)

Right: A forward observation post relays information back to headquarters. The officer in the foreground shows a fairly typical disregard for official uniform dress codes, wearing a white scarf and suede boots. (TR 999)

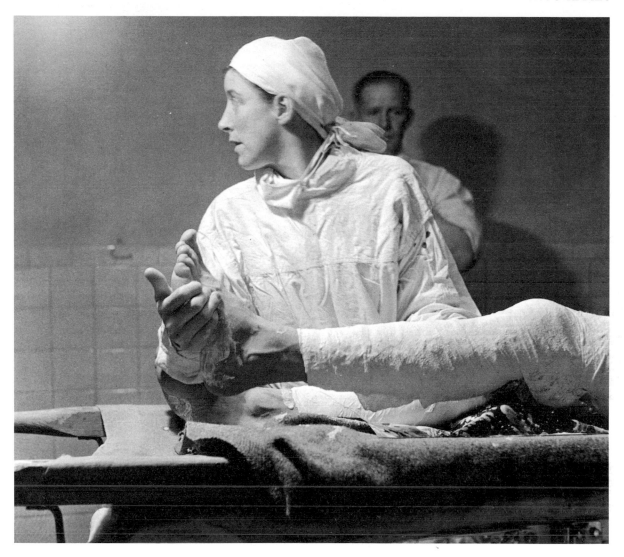

the main demand for medical treatment came from disease: for every battle casualty there would at least twenty men laid low with sickness. The top five complaints (measured in number of cases per 1000) were listed as: digestive system (79), skin diseases (50), dysentery (33), venereal disease (31) and malaria (29). All were curable but the treatment took time and used up resources.

Captain Pleydell's duties as a medical officer included instructing the men under his charge in the rudiments of first aid and the dangers of sexual activity. Pleydell was pleased at the success of his talks:

I am glad to say, I had no cases of VD. My lectures on first aid, splints, etc., were interspersed with lectures on unwise sex, and the effects of VD. I laid it on so thick that two men fainted during one lecture. We were standing up, in the sand, and thump, thump, down they went. Reproachful glances in my direction!

In the desert, stomach complaints were a nuisance and although most

A nurse tends a man with a broken leg in a field hospital in Tobruk. The picture was taken by the famous society photographer Cecil Beaton who undertook a number of foreign assignments during the war. (CBM.1005)

Occupational therapy became increasingly popular in the rehabilitation of severely wounded men during the Desert campaigns. These men are engaged in embroidery. (E.17148)

soldiers suffered to some degree the problem usually sorted itself out fairly quickly. A more persistent problem was that of desert sores. Sergeant John Longstaff of 7th Rifle Brigade explained: 'You only had to scratch yourself and you'd get great festering sores on your legs and knees and fingers.' Successful treatment was difficult, as Pleydell recounted:

Desert sores were commonplace and presumably you were either sensitive or immune to the infection which caused the sore. The official advice in the Army manual was not suitable, and the most effective treatment I found was to cover the sore with strapping or Elastoplast to occlude the oxygen in the air. We spent most of our sick parades treating desert sores which on fingers or hands could make a man unfit for rifle duty. Officers disliked being sent down the line on account of desert sores – it was almost as if they had been demoted.

The flies that clustered around the sores drove the men nearly mad. The eggs laid by the flies in the sores and wounds hatched into maggots, and although unpleasant, devoured the pus and kept the sore clean. Another hazard was that they were susceptible to secondary infections. A good friend of mine developed extensive sores and became infected with diphtheria. I evacuated him to hospital where he was put to bed. He sat up one morning and fell back, dead.

Malaria was not a scourge of the forces in North Africa, unlike the Far East where the successful conduct of military operations could depend on the incidence of the disease. Pools of low-lying water acted as the breeding ground for the malarial mosquito and, of course, these were rare in the desert. The occasional desert oasis proved to be a source of malaria. Pleydell:

I saw only a few cases of malaria, and they were not serious. But at Siwa Oasis, about 100 miles south of Mersa Matruh, I was told that malaria caused so much sickness that an expert had to be sent from the UK to advise. He examined the large pools of water and recommended that they should be stocked with a certain species of fish which would eat the mosquito larvae. His recommendations were put into effect; the larvae were devoured and the malaria ceased. Subsequently, the British garrison was replaced by an Australian force. It did not take the Australians long to appreciate that fish made a welcome addition to their rations, and as the population of fish declined so the malaria sickness rate returned.

Treatment in these isolated spots was rather basic, according to F. G. Harrison of the LRDG: 'Occasionally the Sudanese Defence Force used to come round with a gallon jar of quinine. The dosage was to drink as much as you could before you were sick.' Another LRDG man, Roderick Matthews, summed up his feelings towards health in general: 'Our health was first class. I don't remember anybody being ill, apart from the old gippy tummy. You lived in a very healthy environment.'

PART TWO

THE EIGHTH ARMY ATTACKS

'We couldn't bale out then as there was all hell going round us. The lesser of two evils was to remain in the tank. When night fell, the battle subsided and we found ourselves in the middle of the aerodrome, surrounded by burning tanks – our troops having retreated'.

JAMES FRASER, *8th RTR*

Crusader and the Benghazi Stakes Again

Rommel's daring foray into Cyrenaica in the spring of 1941 had thrown the British out of Libya, leaving the garrison at Tobruk beseiged by the Germans. In Operation Brevity (May 1941) a British force attempted to secure the tactically important Halfaya Pass as a springboard for further offensive action but had been unceremoniously chased back across the frontier. In June a second, larger offensive (Operation Battleaxe) similarly met with failure. Unco-ordinated British tactics were no match for the German panzer formations.

One consequence of the failure of Battleaxe was the replacement of Wavell on 21 June as Commander-in-Chief by General Sir Claude Auchinleck, a highly regarded officer from the Indian Army. The command shake-up was mirrored by other organizational changes, not least the formation of the Eighth Army to take the place of the Western Desert Force. The new Army commander was to be Lieutenant-General Sir Alan Cunningham, the recent victor of British operations in Ethiopia. Under constant pressure from Churchill to launch a new offensive, Auchinleck and Cunningham were forced to draw up a plan of campaign with the utmost rapidity.

Designated Operation Crusader, the British plan called for a major armoured offensive by XXX Corps (Lieutenant-General Willoughby Norrie) to swing round through the desert, take on and destroy the Axis armour and relieve Tobruk. XIII Corps (Lieutenant-General A. R. Godwin-Austen) was primarily an infantry formation. Its role in the coming battle was to sidestep the Axis defences around Halfaya and Sollum and then advance along the coastal strip towards Tobruk and meet up with XXX Corps.

Auchinleck had insisted upon the tightest security and the Germans were unaware of the Eighth Army's preparations. On 18 November 1941 the British tanks advanced into the desert. An intelligence officer in XXX Corps, R. H. Dahl, described the sight of the armour on the move: 'We gazed ahead at scores of widely spaced vehicles – as far as the eye could see – all spewing up their plumes of desert sand. I was suddenly filled with awe at my first glimpse of the sinews of war.'

Taken by surprise, the German reaction was initially slow and confused. At first the Afrika Korps commander assumed that the British armoured offensive was only a reconnaissance. Consequently, XXX Corps' advance was relatively unimpeded until it came upon the Ariete Division at Bir el Gubi and the German defences around the airfield at Sidi Rezegh on 19 November. There the British advance was stopped. The following day the Germans – now fully aware of the situation – launched a major counter-attack against XXX Corps with the 15th and

A British Cruiser Tank Mk VI Crusader passes a burning PzKpfw IV during Operation Crusader. Despite possessing good mobility the Crusader was under-armoured and its 2-pounder gun was clearly inadequate against the German panzers. (E.6751)

21st Panzer Divisions. This was an extraordinarily confused engagement, later known as the 'multi-layered' battle. The fiercest fighting centred around Sidi Rezegh. A crew member of an M3 Stuart light tank, Bob Sykes, found himself caught up in an enormous armoured mêlée as each side fought for control of the airfield:

I cannot describe the confusion of this all-out tank battle; we were here, there and everywhere. I kept switching from tank to tank – out for a breather and some replenishments and back in again. I do not know who was keeping the score but we were losing a great deal of equipment and men. With our light tanks we were weaving in and out of the battle zone, right in the thick of it. We had developed a tactic of going at the back of the German tank where it was only lightly armoured, and piling into it with some pretty disastrous effects to the engine. The noise, the heat and the dust were unbearable.

We were in support of the 8th RTR [Royal Tank Regiment] who were in front of us with heavier tanks but the enemy came in behind us and we were engaged in a fierce battle down to a few hundred yards. We beat them off and continued to assist the 8th RTR but they were later overwhelmed by the onslaught while we had to retire as we were low on octane and ammo.

James Fraser was a tank crewman in the 8th RTR and won the Military Medal at Sidi Rezegh. Later he earned fame as Montgomery's tank driver. Here he recounts the fighting on 22 November 1941:

We were doing an attack on the Sidi Rezegh aerodrome. We were equipped with Valentine tanks with a three-man crew, of which I was the driver, plus an officer named Pete Kitto and the gunner, a lad from Skipton. We were armed with two-pounder guns but they were useless against the German tanks. We'd come under heavy fire and my tank was engaged on the side but it must have been a glancing blow – it didn't do any damage. I swung around and an

Sergeant James Fraser (second left) poses for the camera in a photograph taken during the Alamein period, when he had transferred to the 6th RTR (and a Grant tank) to act as driver for Montgomery (right). The Eighth Army commander's distinctive tanker's beret was donated to him by Fraser. (E.19096)

armour-piercing shell went through the back of the tank, right into the engine, and stopped it. Fortunately the engine was diesel and there was no fire, unlike a Grant tank which, with its high-octane petrol, was like a mobile crematorium – as soon as it was hit it would just go up and explode like a tin of bully beef.

We couldn't bale out then as there was all hell going round us. The lesser of the two evils was to remain in the tank. When night fell, the battle subsided and we found ourselves in the middle of the aerodrome, surrounded by burning tanks – our troops having retreated. We had faint wireless contact with our HQ squadron but this died out. We settled down for the night within the tank itself.

In the morning Pete Kitto stood on top of the turret with his binoculars to have a look around to see what was happening. An anti-tank rifle fired and chipped half his knee away. He was badly wounded. We put a tourniquet on it. By virtue of my seniority as a lance-corporal I had to take charge. I thought the only thing we could do was to try and make contact with our own lines.

In getting away we came under a hell of a lot of small-arms fire, but we were dead lucky and got away. After a day of carrying Kitto we came across some troops on the horizon. It looked to me like German armoured cars and I went on to a ridge to investigate. Much to my delight and surprise it was a South African armoured car. Pete Kitto was immediately taken to hospital, where he survived. I was transferred back to my own unit and picked up another tank.

In two days of battle the Afrika Korps had brought XXX Corps's advance to a standstill and broken its offensive capability. The only ray of hope lay in the advance of XIII Corps. While the 4th Indian Division

Men of the 4th Indian Division chalk a cheery slogan on to their lorry, a device favoured by war photographers to demonstrate the robust good humour and high morale of the troops at the front. Hellfire Pass was the nickname for Halfaya Pass, a strong position on the Libyan escarpment, which was held by the Germans until the eventual success of Operation Crusader. (E.3660)

pinned down the Axis front line between Sollum and Sidi Omar, the New Zealand Division had made good progress and was advancing towards Tobruk. But even here lay danger: if the Afrika Korps turned away northwards from its battle with the British armour the isolated New Zealanders would be destroyed. It was a moment of crisis in the British camp.

Cunningham's early optimism had completely evaporated and, exhausted by the strain of command, he contemplated withdrawal. Auchinleck flew up to confer with his generals and took direct command of the battle. Although the Eighth Army had taken a battering it was not a defeated force and Auchinleck realized that the Germans too had suffered heavy casualties.

As Auchinleck was taking stock of the British situation, events took a new turn. Rather than continue the battle to destroy XXX Corps, Rommel impetuously led his forces directly westward in an attempt to cut the British supply lines along the frontier wire. Rommel's 'dash to the wire' proved a costly mistake. Under Auchinleck's leadership the British held firm. The Axis forces were repulsed and, short of petrol and supplies, they were forced to retreat in order to prevent XIII Corps linking up with the defenders in Tobruk.

Halfaya pass – better known to the troops as Hellfire pass – was a scene of fighting between German armour and the 2nd South African Division. A patrol of South African armoured cars came across a suspicious column of vehicles. A soldier was sent on ahead to investigate:

I went forward to identify the column which was very difficult as they had so many of the type of vehicles we used ourselves. I couldn't be sure until over three parts of the way there. Just as I recognized them as the enemy I found I was looking down the barrel of a pistol held in the hand of the fiercest specimen of humanity it has been my misfortune to lay eyes on. Seeing it was hopeless to make a dash back to the cars I threw up my hands, which was also the pre-arranged signal for the cars to make off.

All hell was let loose as Jerry opened up with all he had, but thanks to the skill of our drivers I could see they'd got away safely. This made the enemy officers more annoyed than ever and I was subjected to some pretty severe bullying. But having seen the job successfully carried out it never worried me.

The South African soldier was taken down with other prisoners into captivity in a cave near Halfaya Pass. They were subsequently rescued when the British captured the position.

South-west of Halfaya the 4th Indian Division had been engaged with Axis forces. M. E. Parker was a subaltern in an anti-tank battery of the 65th (Norfolk Yeomanry) Artillery Regiment:

Our objective was Sidi Omar which is where the International Wire takes a turn southwards. We were supported by 42 RTR in Matildas, most of which were written off by German 88s in the initial assault. The 88s were in turn shot up by a 25-pounder which was wheeled up and which took them on over open sights. It took three days to capture Sidi Omar: we held one half and the Italians, plus German gunners, the other.

It was decided to concentrate a 'stonk' on the remaining portion. The barrage was by no means small and when it was over a considerable number of Italians had had enough and surrendered. The following day after a repeat performance – before the final assault – an Italian came in and apologized for being late in surrendering. He explained that he had been asleep! I thought to myself if we are expected to believe that then we will believe anything – how could anyone sleep through that lot? I was wrong as I later found out for myself.

In the final assault the Indians in their Bren carriers whistled all over the trenches, lobbing in pineapples [grenades] to some effect.

Although the Germans were far from beaten the tide of battle had turned in favour of the British. Auchinleck decided to continue the offensive. Having lost faith in Cunningham, Auchinleck reluctantly relieved him of his command on 26 November, choosing as his replacement his Deputy Chief-of-Staff, Lieutenant-General Neil Ritchie.

The focus of the battle once again swung back to the area between Sidi Rezegh and the Tobruk perimeter. The German 'dash to the wire' had given time for XXX Corps to reorganize itself and it returned to the fray. During the first week in December the Germans fought desperately to dislodge the British from their forward positions near Tobruk. On 7 December, short of petrol and ammunition, Rommel admitted defeat and decided to withdraw his forces – still largely intact – rather than risk destruction by continuing the battle. During the rest of December the Germans skilfully withdrew from Cyrenaica, the British pursuit hampered by poor weather and the exhaustion of their forces.

Both Axis and British armies had been of a similar size (around

The Commander-in-Chief General Sir Claude Auchinleck (left) discusses the tactical situation with the new Eighth Army commander Lieutenant-General Neil Ritchie (centre), 10 December 1941. (E.6945)

Tobruk link-up: Brigadier A. C. Willison (right), commanding 32nd Armoured Brigade based in Tobruk, greets Lieutenant-Colonel S. E. Hartnell, OC of 19th New Zealand Infantry Battalion, 2 December 1941. The New Zealand Division's advance along the coastal strip was one of the outstanding features of Operation Crusader. (E.6893)

110,000 men each) but casualty figures favoured the British with 18,000 as against 38,000 for the Axis, many of them captured during the retreat from Cyrenaica. A major consequence of the battle had been the relief of Tobruk. While Auchinleck could take satisfaction in having thrown the Germans out of Cyrenaica his victory was none the less indecisive: the Afrika Korps had survived to fight another day, and with the arrival of reinforcements early in January 1942 it was ready to recommence the battle.

The British position was weakened by the withdrawal of experienced British and Australian formations to the Far East, following Japan's entry into the war on 7 December 1941. Like Wavell before him, Auchinleck suddenly saw his army denuded while stretched out across the Cyrenaican bulge. Rommel was fully aware of the British problems and he struck on 21 January. His two panzer divisions had been reinforced by the arrival of the mechanized 90th Light Division – which soon proved to be another elite formation.

The inexperienced and scattered British 1st Armoured Division was brushed aside as the Axis divisions raced forward into the bulge of Cyrenaica, in a repeat performance of the spring offensive the previous year. Lieutenant D. F. Parry was the workshop commander of an anti-aircraft battery based in Benghazi:

It took over twenty-four hours for the news of the disaster in the south to filter through to Benghazi, and as always the news was played down: 'There has been a slight penetration of our lines at Sirte but necessary measures are being taken to restore the situation.' This was followed by: 'It has been found necessary to form defensive positions to the east of Sirte; however, the situation is stabilizing and Benghazi is not in any danger.' Some days later: 'as a precautionary measure steps will be taken to evacuate Benghazi', followed by 'your workshop will leave Benghazi and proceed to Tobruk'.

Parry got out just in time: on 29 January German forces entered the town. Although caught by surprise at the speed of Rommel's advance the British withdrawal was for the most part orderly. While Rommel consolidated his new gains the British fell back on fortified positions along a line from Gazala on the coast to the desert outpost of Bir Hakeim. This would be the next battleground in the Desert War.

Eighth Army Style

In military institutions a man identifies himself with small groups: his squad or section, his company and at the furthest extreme his battalion or regiment. Brigades, divisions and armies are too distant and amorphous to provide much emotional hold over the common soldier. Sometimes there are exceptions, and the Eighth Army was one.

For over two years the Eighth Army had been stationed in one specific and far-flung theatre of war. At first, troops in North Africa felt themselves ignored by those back in Britain; the initials MEF (Middle East Force) were known as 'Men England Forgot'. Over time, this isolation helped form special customs, habits and slang, in effect a special Eighth Army style.

The fact that the army in North Africa was the only British military force fighting the Germans during this period gave extra kudos to being a 'Desert Rat'. After Rommel's defeat at Alamein the desert veterans began to affect a note of contempt for outsiders, including the troops of the First Army, newly sent out from Britain and dubbed 'those bloody Ingleses'. James Fraser – a Royal Tank Regiment driver – summed up the exclusivity and comradeship of the Eighth Army:

Complete with sola topees and 'Bombay Bloomers' a column of newly arrived British infantry marches along a road in Egypt to begin the process of 'getting their knees brown'. (E.4735)

61

Somewhat bloodied but
certainly not bowed, two
wounded Australian
infantrymen light up after a
dawn patrol around Tobruk,
12 September 1941. After
several months in the field the
desert rat dress began to
resemble the battered yet
practical uniform illustrated
here. (E.5506)

Among the desert troops there was a sort of affinity. When people came out
from England – had not got their knees brown – you looked on them, irrespec-
tive of what experience they had, as interlopers until they proved themselves. If
there was ever a club then the desert squaddies of all units were a club on their
own. Whenever you went on leave you never drank in a bar on your own.
Whether it was an infantryman from the Rifle Brigade or whatever, they would
join you.

Desert conditions demanded appropriate uniforms. What the authorities prescribed and what was actually worn were often two different
things. Troops would arrive in Egypt in regulation tropical kit – complete with sola topees and baggy shorts – and through time and with
experience develop their own, more sensible response to the environment. Rifleman Frederick Jones explained: 'In the desert nobody's
smart. When you've been in the desert for two or three years, parade-
ground elegance goes by the board.'

Jack Daniel had been issued with standard tropical kit for service in
the Middle East, and along with tens of thousands of other fellow
unfortunates he had a pretty poor opinion of it:

We had these ridiculous sunhats, and these trousers which we used to call
shit-stoppers. Some designer had made these shorts in such a way that they
doubled up and were buttoned on each side with the idea that they could be
lowered at night to be long trousers – to avoid mosquitos and tsetse files. Well
this never occurred to us, as with so much other equipment in the army. But
what did occur to us, is that because they weren't exactly flush with the shorts
you walked around with these balloons at your feet, which the troops immediately called shit-stoppers.

Officers had more latitude in what they wore and this led to some decidedly non-regulation uniforms, made famous in the cartoons of Jon's Two Types, which affectionately parodied the sartorial extravagances of the two captains, Fortescue and ffoulkes.

A certain level of eccentricity in the way an officer dressed was seen as the badge of an old desert hand. Hugh Daniel noted: 'It's no exaggeration that they were flamboyant and the troops loved it, they wanted something to identify themselves with and to look at. Perhaps that's why Montgomery made such a mark when he wore a black beret and an Australian bush hat – the men liked to identify with something other than the strict uniform.' This Eighth Army style quickly communicated itself to new arrivals. L. E. Tutt wryly observed the sudden and startling transformation of the officers in his yeomanry regiment as they entered Egypt from Palestine:

We noticed that a strange change had taken place in our officers since we had crossed the Suez Canal. They had suddenly abandoned all pose of being cavalry officers. They all began to wear khaki drill, which their batmen prematurely aged by washing it and covering in sand as it dried. They all took the stiffeners out of their caps and crushed them into impossible shapes. It also became *de rigueur* to wear desert boots, irreverently described by other ranks as 'brothel creepers', and to carry a fly whisk with a short leather-covered handle and a brush of violently coloured horse hair. In their kits, instead of a field-marshal's baton, they carried a brightly coloured cravat – they all had one to wear when it became the 'thing'. Years later we were to laugh at the cartoonist Jon's Two Types. They could well have been based on our officers.

Another distinctive feature of Eighth Army style was the jargon used by the troops. Trooper Kenneth Morris was fascinated by this slang:

All conversations were heavily enriched with Arabic. It distinguished veterans from rookies, insiders from those who 'did not have their knees brown'. It was not just features like wadi (dried up river bed) or everyday words like 'shai' (tea) or 'bint' (girl), even 'sar kam da watti?' was preferred to 'What time is it?' The philosophy of the desert was best reflected in 'alakeefic' (couldn't care less), 'marleesh' (it doesn't matter) and 'bar dinn' (sometime – later rather than sooner). In time I absorbed over seventy words and phrases to impress later arrivals.

The pride in using Arabic was also exemplified in the occasional singsong when the canteen truck received a rare issue of cans of warm light beer. An old soldier might recall sad ditties from the Irish troubles of the Twenties. Then most would join in singing a mournful ballad about 'a bunch of violets blue'. But the favourite song was 'Saida Bint' [Hello Girl], which happily combined bilingual familiarity with dreams of dalliance in Cairo.

The journalist Godfrey Talbot was amused by the Eighth Army's jargon, comparing it to the British soldier's French approximations in the First World War:

Where the soldier in the last war – wanting to say something wasn't good – would say 'no bon', the soldiers out here say 'mush kye-ee'. And if a wandering Arab comes along scrounging for sugar and you haven't much, you say, 'mafish

Two British officers compare their sheepskin coats, which during the winter were as *de rigeur* as brothel creepers. Sartorial eccentricity became an Eighth Army trademark as the Desert War progressed. (E.21517)

sooka' [mafish, no more; sooka, sugar] Again, a soldier from the Eighth Army will say, 'Come and have a shufti [look]'. The Arabic word for one is 'wha-hid' and the word for street or road is 'sharia', and in a bar you'll hear these words laboriously brought in, as one man says to the other: 'Let's have wha-hid for the sharia'.

Apart from the Arabic there are various phrases which have become catch words. If a thing is satisfactory, it is 'just the job'. Another popular saying to be used incongruously whenever possible is one I heard when we were getting up after a bit of bombing; a soldier who'd been flattened on the ground looked up at the grey smoke clouds of the bomb, grinned and said, 'There's no future in this.'

Out of the Line

During the Second World War the Army High Command recognized the need to rotate their front-line units at regular intervals; without some form of rest and relaxation the fighting efficiency of the troops would be seriously impaired. For the men of the Eighth Army this meant a chance to get out of the desert and return to some form of civilization, either in Alexandria or more usually Cairo.

In an age before foreign travel was commonplace – except for the rich – countries like Egypt held a special allure to the average Briton. For tens of thousands of British and Commonwealth troops the experience of Cairo left an indelible memory. To old soldiers, Egypt was known as 'the land of the four 'S's – Sun, Sand, Sin and Syphilis'. Many of the men of the Eighth Army would find this motto equally true of their time in North Africa. Gunner L. E. Tutt provided this vivid description of Cairo:

To me it was one of the great cities of the world. It is a great sprawl of a place, jam packed with Cairenes who have had enough of their mud villages. They crowd the pavements, the shops, the bazaars. They pile on to the noisy trams and flood the open-fronted cafés.

The city mounts a direct assault on all the senses. It bombards the eyes, the ears, the nose and the nerve endings with a plethora of experiences, all of them new, all of them exciting and stimulating. Its critics say that it smells to high heaven in the summer. It doesn't, it smells to high heaven all the year round. But the reek is of living people. It's the gutsy smell of peasants cooking their kuftas and kebabs, and roasting ears of corn over early morning charcoal braziers. It's the smell of the Nile, water highway and lifeline cum sewer. It is the smell of damp apartments and freshly ironed gelabas; the acrid whiff of Egyptian tobacco with strong undertones of hashish.

It is a noisy city, but why whisper when you can shout? People laughing and loving and living should do it at the top of their voices. The trams clang and clatter, their conductors blowing little pip squeaks of hunting horns. From every café comes the clatter of backgammon pieces, the gurgle of water pipe and in the background the nasal, off-pitch singing from a radio.

The city itself mounts an attack on the vision. Tall buildings with their neon signs. The purple Bougainvillaca slashing the green of Gezira. White houses, hung with violent red peppers drying in the sun. Black-robed women, shapeless and sexless, until you catch the whiff of a Paris perfume. For nine months we had lived in a dust-coloured world, our noses full of the stench of cordite and the oily fumes from burning vehicles. We were starved of visual and tactile experiences, but our pockets were full of money and we intended to live like kings.

Out of the line, a phlegmatic-looking Australian undergoes the attentions of the tattooist's needle. Acquiring an impressive collection of tattoos was (and still is) one of the initiation rites of a soldier. (E.20924)

Once a soldier had arrived in Cairo the important thing was to get the desert out of his system. For Hugh Daniel: 'A bath was the great thing to sit and soak in; it was absolute bliss.' Once cleaned up the soldier could spend his period of leave – often no more than four or five days in the city – on entertainment. Tutt describes how he and his friends set about preparing themselves for the coming treat, at times with scant regard to King's Regulations:

We found hotels; no leave camps for us. We tipped extravagantly, under the impression that it would get us better rooms. It didn't. We threw our side packs into a corner and bounced appreciatively on our beds. At least we were prudent enough to pay for our rooms in advance. Whatever happened we would have a place to sleep. Next, the barber's shop where we sat in our chairs and went through the card – shave, shampoo, haircut, friction massage, hot towels and manicure. The bowl ran brown with the accumulated dirt in our scalps, the sand gritted on the scissors and the hot towels came away like mud packs.

By the time we called for a taxi we were beginning to feel human again. The tailor treated us with the deference of a man who hears his cash register ringing. We stepped out of the khaki drill that we had arrived in and ordered bush jackets and slacks cut from officer's material and tailored to fit. After only slight deliberation we promoted ourselves to the rank of sergeant. We considered commissioned rank but sergeants really do get better treatment than officers, at least in the sort of places in which we were likely to find ourselves. One of our

The reading room of the Corner Club in Cairo, a services club reserved for sergeants and warrant officers. The military authorities were understandably keen to promote such well-ordered activities. The seedy bars and brothels of the Berka district were strictly off-limits to photographers. (E.11658)

junior officers was at the bar in Shepheard's when he realized that the agreeable captain talking to the group at his elbow was our sergeant in charge of fitters. But he was a good sport and they bought one another a drink before going their separate ways. John Pounds, our signals NCO, spent the whole of one leave as a lieutenant-colonel, but we all felt that was going over the top a bit.

The first couple of days were frenetic. We dined in the best restaurants, although Cairo has never been cordon bleu country, despite the influence of the French. We shuttled about in taxis from bar to bar, to Groppi's, to the Blue Nile Cabaret. Never stopping in one place for very long, always the urge to take another taxi, to move to another place. We were suffering from a well-known complaint – 'leave fever' – and we had to get it out of our systems before we could settle down to enjoy our leave quietly.

Whenever we entered a cabaret the cherry brandy bints would come crowding round, girls who wanted to sit and talk with lonely soldiers, provided they bought them cherry brandies with monotonous frequency. After one disastrous evening of getting drunk on liqueurs we stuck to ice-cold beer. Late one night though, we were tempted into trying the deadly Zebeeb, the Egyptian cousin of Ouzo, Raki and Arak. We poured a libation of water into our glasses, and watched the clear spirit turn as clouded as our befuddled brains.

Drinking was one of the rituals of leave in Cairo, a chance to blow an accumulation of back pay and a means to escape the tedium of life in the desert. D. A. Main recalled one particularly heavy session:

On the second night in Cairo it was suggested that we try to drink our way through the alphabet of the Pole du Nord. A referred to anisette, B for beer, C for cider and so on. Unfortunately we could only drink as far as H then we went to Groppi's where we obtained sticky pastries, and more important, further alcohol. My two friends had consumed six whiskies each but I had abstained. However, they mentioned that we all might be dead within a few days and I was invited to join them – so I had six whiskies whilst they had a further six. They were both killed within a few days. I vaguely remember returning to our quarters.

Not surprisingly drinking at these levels by young men – often fresh out of combat – led to serious disturbances. One more minor form of civil commotion was the widespread practice of soldiers taking over the horse-drawn taxis or gharries for their own amusement. 'When you had rival groups of men,' noted Hugh Daniel, 'say from a tank regiment or one of the armoured brigades coming into Cairo they'd hire these gharries, the driver would be persuaded to get in the back and the lads would get on the jockey seat and race around, frightening onlookers.'

Inter-service rivalries often came to a head, particularly between the RAF and the Army. Harold Fitzjohn:

At one time we weren't fighting the Germans, we were fighting the RAF. Fighting would break out in pubs in Alex and Cairo, and it was always against some poor RAF chap. They were blamed for the absence of aircraft over the battlefield. The soldiers would call out: 'Where the hell are you – you're never there!' Drinking sparked off the fights; people on leave from the desert with a lot of beer down them. There was plenty of fisticuffs, and with a few more involved it was practically a riot.

There were also a lot of bar-room brawls, often occasioned by the soldiers real or imagined belief that they were being fleeced by the civilian population. Regardless of the rights and wrongs of the situation, the military authorities were quick to stamp on street violence. Kenneth Morris was temporarily assigned to help the Military Police in Cairo:

We were transported to the MP barracks at Bab el Hadid and paraded with the police. To enable us to assert our authority, which we did not feel, we were given piquet armbands. On the parade we were rather overawed by the heavily blancoed equipment of the regular police but in town they became more fraternal. Our job was to close down any troublesome cabarets and run in any drunks. The early patrols were expected to be quiet and consisted of two piquets and one MP. We kept a very close eye on our MP to avoid getting lost; we would have had little idea of where to find the guardroom.

The MP led us into a pension – probably the Union Jack – where we were greeted by the smiling Greek proprietor who seated us at a small table. The MP ordered 'the usual all round' – egg and chips. There was no question of payment. I had much to learn.

The evening wore on. Around midnight an urgent request came from the Sweet Melody Cabaret. With the MPs and other volunteers from the piquet we found the place in an uproar. Glass littered the floor and bottles were flying. One soldier thumped a piano unmelodiously, another banged a drum. Four danced the Palais Glide on a wooden stage. Flustered cabaret girls darted

South African troops crowd round to watch a water polo match at the Springbok Club, Helwan. The Commonwealth forces had their own special recreational centres where troops could relax, away from the temptations of heavy drinking and prostitution. (E.12007)

hither and thither. Every group of soldiers sang something different but fortunately most left the hall with little more than a protest, though some of the Scots needed careful handling. My education in Cairo life was continuing apace.

Back in the guardroom we learnt that a further SOS from a café whose diners had staged a sit-down strike had been settled. In the streets groups passed by singing merrily but we quietened only the more rowdy and arrested nobody. Peace descended on the neighbourhood.

If heavy drinking was an acceptable (because only occasional) nuisance, the military authorities were more concerned about the troops' sexual behaviour. Extra-marital sex in the 1940s was still a matter of moral confusion: powerful groups of do-gooders in Britain campaigned tirelessly to prevent the men having access to sex. Although these moral guardians had some success in closing down brothels and limiting the availability of condoms to the troops, the Army saw the problem primarily from a medical angle.

Wherever armed forces went so prostitution followed, and the authorities reluctantly conceded that it would be impossible to prevent sex. The question was how to control it and prevent the spread of venereal disease. VD was a major problem for the Army: the number of reported cases of the disease in the Middle East for 1941 and '42 were

The official caption reads: 'The boys are all eyes and smiles as Carol of Stockton-on-Tees hands out "Kumangetit" Fund comforts at Mena, where they are on their way to the front.' Carol was one of three ENSA glamour girls who toured the base camps handing out 'cigarettes and cordials' to the troops. (E.14917)

always higher than battle casualties. And as treatment for infected soldiers took them out of their units for three weeks or more, this had serious consequences for front-line divisions chronically short of manpower.

The Army's solution was to provide the troops with information on the dangers of the disease (which if caught could lead to loss of pay) and the setting up of controlled red light districts where the prostitutes underwent regular medical checks. The brothels set aside for the other ranks were very basic affairs, where sex was dispensed on a conveyor-belt principle with little or no regard to the formalities of romance. None the less they held a fascination for the troops, even at second hand. Harold Fitzjohn:

Troops did use brothels but they were absolute filth. I considered my health more important than to go into places like that. In Alexandria you'd go to Sister Street for the brothel area and in Cairo it was the Berka.

If one of the lads was daft enough to go with one of the girls, the old Madame would charge the others with him a few piastres. Then they'd walk along a corridor to where there were pinholes in the wall, and they could look through them and watch their friend in action – much to his anger when he came out.

Such reticence is fairly typical of the stories related by most Eighth

Army soldiers. Another similar though fuller account comes from L. E. Tutt:

We made our obligatory visit to the Berka, the brothel area. We would have been branded as lacking in some way had we ever confessed that we had never even seen the place. I cannot imagine any place less likely to arouse the passions. Great echoing houses with stone staircases, reeking of urine and Condy's disinfectant. There was a queue at every door. As the girls ushered one man out and the next one in, they called: 'Be quick. Very, very busy today.' But the line at each door didn't grow any shorter.

Occasionally a girl would stand for a moment to beg a cigarette and get a breather. Sweat-stained and dressed in tawdry rags they were less than feminine. They exchanged badinage with their waiting clients and got involved in hair-tearing fights if they thought that another girl was taking one of their 'regulars'. The onlookers would cheer them on to greater efforts until a Madame would come swearing out of her room to slap them into submission. They returned to their rooms, still spitting and snarling at one another. Then it was back to business.

Sometimes the next in line would look through the keyhole and deliver a running commentary to those behind him, and shout to the couple inside 'Come on. Get on with it.' Those right at the end of the queue sang the traditional complaint of the soldier, 'Why are we waiting, always bloody well waiting'.

Quiet, mouselike little girls of about eight or nine years old stole in and out of rooms with fresh supplies of towels and disinfectants, or a message from Madame that the girls were taking too long. The young ones were apprentices, just waiting until they could become 'proper' girls, with a room of their own and their own clients.

James Witte, a gunner in the Essex Yeomanry, was rather less inhibited when describing his red light adventures:

Sharia il Berka, the street of the brothels, opened for business precisely at two o'clock in the afternoon. It carried on until the MPs dragged away the last reluctant drunk. (It was amazing the number of soldiers who had to get tanked-up before they visited a brothel.) Berka Street was situated almost opposite the fashionable Shepheard's Hotel which was 'off-limits' to other ranks. It was a place where officers met their lady friends: not having their money or their opportunities, we made use of the Berka, not only for the purposes of fornication but to sit and chat with your fellow men and eye the girls as they took customers to their rooms.

I soon found out that it was best to be stone-cold sober when you went to a brothel. The girls really detested drunks and I can't say I blamed them. Each brothel had a number; some were better patronized than others. Each had a Madame in charge of the girls, usually a prostitute who had moved from the bed to the cash desk. One such Madame was known as Tiger Lil and it was her proud boast that she had served our fathers and that she was prepared to serve us. Most soldiers, especially the inexperienced, went for the young, good-looking 'bints', but the older hands said that it was better to select one who was older and more experienced.

Whoever you went with you still ran the risks of 'copping a packet', despite

71

the fact that Army doctors regularly inspected the girls. To lessen the risk of venereal disease, it was advisable to visit the PAC [Prophylactic Ablution Centre] and take the necessary precautions, which consisted of squirting a solution of permanganate potash crystals up the penis. After this the customer collected a blue ticket on the way out which guaranteed him no loss of pay if he contracted gonorrhoea or syphilis. But, of course, the only real preventive measure was total abstinence. A visit to Cairo's Hygiene Museum was one of the finest ways of ensuring abstinence. Here in a large room was a remarkable collection of plaster casts of male sexual organs in every stage of gonorrhoea and syphilis. An hour here dispelled all thoughts of going with the birds. But despite such grim warnings the brothels of Cairo did a roaring trade.

You went up the stairs and sat down in company with dozens of other customers and sightseers. Each girl had her own gimmick to attract custom. But the best gimmick was youth and beauty. Many of us succumbed to their blandishments, forgetting about the Hygiene Museum, and we disappeared upstairs to reappear ten minutes later looking rather sheepish.

The British soldier's enthusiasm for 'booze 'n' bints' was not universal, however. Louis Challoner, a gunner from the 2nd Regiment RHA, took a censorious view of the boorish behaviour of his fellow countryman abroad:

The ordinary soldier's lack of imagination and dullness of perception are nowhere so noticeable in such places as Cairo. With unfailing regularity he seeks out the dingiest dance hall or cabaret and proceeds to get drunk on imported, expensive American canned beer. There is a type of British soldier who is not happy at a dance unless he is tight. Failing that, he seeks out a restaurant where 'English Cooking' is advertised and stuffs himself with egg and chips, all the while insulting the entire population of the rest of the world in a loud voice for their habit of eating unaccustomed food.

Other soldiers took their tourism in a more restrained way. H. A. Wilson decided to visit the wonders of ancient Egypt. There, however, he found the entrepreneurial activities of the present-day Egyptian tiresome:

Caught a lorry to Mena and visited the Pyramids. The site was crawling with Wogs [an acronym for Westernized Oriental Gentlemen, then a slightly less pejorative word than it is today] and they all saw me coming. Many had asses, horses or mules and wanted to carry me for so many piastres but I shoo'd them away. One cute, smooth-tongued fellow clung to me like a leech, however, and I let him show me around, not because I really needed a guide but because he kept the others away.

Wasn't really interested in all the Gizeh masonry but the Sphinx impressed me. I stood for ten minutes in front of it trying to read the riddle in its face. Inside the Great Pyramid the guide's candle disclosed little of tremendous interest, and when the candle went out and the guide demanded another ten piastres to light a new one I decided it was time to leave.

Despite the inconveniences, Kenneth Morris enjoyed his encounters with the local population:

I caught the tram at the barrack gates for the half-hour journey into Cairo. The large city was an intriguing mixture of old and new, east and west, civil and

The Sphinx endures the gaze of a group of ATS girls sightseeing in Cairo, while Egyptian tradesmen carry on the age-old task of hawking camel rides to the tourist. (E.18609)

military. I was fascinated by the clanging trams, with passengers holding on to every jutting spur and the conductor swinging along the outside collecting fares, the jostling cosmopolitan crowds and the pestering street traders seeking negotiated bargains.

Once a persistent Arab pursued me for an hour, even into a café, offering me attachable sun-glasses at ever lower prices after I had showed a passing interest. I succumbed eventually. There was also an army of small dirty children who earned a doubtful income as boot blacks.

For two evenings I acted the keen tourist. I had an hour's drive round in the splendour of a gharry, passing the palace of King Farouk and the green oasis of Gezira. The next evening I visited the Citadel and three famous mosques; to enter a mosque we had to wear overshoes as an alternative to removing our easily stolen army boots. On one occasion a beggar asking for baksheesh, as usual for his numerous family, was taken aback to hear that I had four wives and seven children – and only murmured 'Great man' in recognition that I was a bigger liar than he.

Men of a tank crew, whose Grant tank prepares to move up the line on a railway flat-bed truck, buy oranges from an Arab boy. (E.9922)

For the 'officer class' leave was generally a more refined business than for the other ranks. Theodore Stephanides was a cosmopolitan figure who enjoyed his chance to escape from the war and meet up with old friends:

It was wonderful to get up in the morning when one felt inclined, to have a hot bath and a good breakfast, to visit the bookshops and to have tea or dinner with pleasant company. I learned that Lawrence and Nancy Durrell [old friends from Corfu] had escaped safely from Greece and were now in Cairo.

Lawrence Durrell spent much of the war in Egypt, gaining the raw material for his celebrated Alexandria Quartet novels. He describes the intellectual life in this period:

Just outside Cairo there was a place called the Anglo-Egyptian Union which was really an officers' club. It was awfully cosmopolitan in the sense that all the Egyptian Army officers were there and the poets, writers and painters would sit in with them. Egypt had not seen an intellectual renaissance like it. The Free French forces brought all their poets and painters with them, as did the British. All of a sudden intellectual movements were starting: I began a poetry rag and five or six now well-known poets contributed to it. This was all a part of the war but very definitely unique in the sense that everything like it had been snuffed out in Europe.

For officers Cairo was a beacon you could fall back on. At one point when the war was only fifty miles away [July-October 1942] you could get back to Cairo from the front in 55 minutes. There you rang up people, you went out to dinner and on Monday morning you had your flask of whisky and were back in the line.

The summer of 1942 was the only time the war really came close to the urban areas of Egypt. When the first news of the German advance reached Cairo and Alexandria on 4 July there was a period of near panic: so many documents were being consigned to the flames in embassy gardens that it became known as 'Ash Wednesday'. The journalist Rex Keating was based in Cairo:

Foreign civilians and most of the British officials in Cairo were evacuated to Palestine. I remained since the radio programme had to be kept going. It was an eerie feeling being alone and abandoned. I was handed the key to the film vaults and a stationwagon loaded to the roof with tins of petrol. By this time we had accumulated a vast footage of film which would have been of great value to the Germans. If the worst happened I was to set fire to the film stock and then beat it south in the stationwagon to Upper Egypt and the Sudan.

Well, as we all know, it never happened but during those four months Cairo was a strange place to be. As if by magic the plaster busts of Churchill hawked around the streets were replaced by ones of Mussolini. Things went for sale at knock down prices. A friend bought a magnificent grand piano for five pounds. Houses, apartment and cars went for a song.

Captain Richard Bromley-Gardener comments on the pro-Axis feelings of the local population, but unlike most British soldiers he got on well with the Egyptians:

During the period leading up to Alamein in the summer of '42, I believe – although I didn't meet much of it myself – that a lot of the poorer elements of Egyptian society became very anti-British and pro-Italian and pro-German. They thought we were on the way out and that they had better support the winning side. But that was soon reversed after Alamein.

I got to know the Egyptians and liked them very much. I liked their wide variety of interests in music and life in general. Of course Cairo was a sophisticated city, very smart and chic. After England, which was beginning to feel the effects of the war, to go abroad anywhere was good and in Cairo and Alexandria they were carrying on as though it was pre-war civilian life.

Bromley-Gardener's open approach was in marked contrast to the general colonial attitude of the British, who for the most part openly despised the Egyptians. Stephanides thought the British were storing up trouble for the future:

I found Egyptians of all classes very helpful and obliging if treated with ordinary politeness – a thing which they rarely got from the occupying forces, at least as far as the lower ranks were concerned. This did immense harm to British interests, both present and future, a subject that did not seem to be sufficiently appreciated by the higher authorities.

A British soldier sips a cup of Turkish coffee alongside a street vendor. Relations between the British and the Egyptian civilian population were, with few exceptions, confined to financial and material exchange. (E.8812)

The ordinary British soldier had a less exalted view of the Egyptian people, perhaps reflecting different experiences of contact, as in Harold Fitzjohn's comment:

To me they were more amusing than anything else. You'd go out one night and you'd be talking to a friend and be aware of something touching your foot. Looking down there'd be a little Arab boy: he'd cleaned one of your shoes until it shone like a mirror while the other one was left covered in dust. And his hands were out for the piastres to do the other shoe. They were very good at making money.

The ubiquitous boot blacks were an occupational hazard of life in the city. Frederick Jones found one boy's tactics less than acceptable, an incident which perhaps coloured his view of Egyptians in general:

A boot-black boy cleaned my boots, just around the corner from the main road. When I was ready to pay him the two ackers [piastres] – or whatever the charge was – he suddenly opened the lid of his liquid black polish and said: 'Two pounds, or I'll cover you in this'. But he wasn't quite quick enough: I'd got one foot on the ground and I pushed him over with the other. Then I quickly got round the corner into the main road, leaving him behind.

The Egyptians were out for whatever they could get, from your paybook (which they could sell to deserters) to cleaning your boots whether they needed it or not. You didn't socialize with the Egyptian people at all.

On arrival in Egypt, Harold Sell had to increase his battalion's security measures to prevent theft on a large scale by the local population:

We had to throw a perimeter around the camps and drive round them in vehicles fitted with miniature searchlights and Bren guns to deal with the marauding Egyptians who were always running around thieving. They were mainly looking for things like rifles, which they were very adept in stealing. A man could put his rifle down with a chain around it and he could wake up the next morning and find it gone. So it was quite necessary to have these aggressive patrols who would fire at them without any hesitation.

The gulf between the Egyptians and the British was wide and in the 1940s unbridgeable. This division was noticed by the more aware British soldiers, but there was little they could do. Fitzjohn concludes this section with a telling anecdote:

During time off the troops would often go to the cinemas, the audience comprising 90 per cent British troops and 10 per cent educated Egyptians, in European suits and red fezes. They'd play 'God Save the King' which everyone stood up for – including the Egyptians – then they'd play the Egyptian National Anthem. At this the soldiers used to sing about the Egyptian king: 'King Farouk, King Farouk/He's one of those and a crook'. I never saw any fights or arguments but I've often wondered what those Egyptians thought of it. That's one thing I was actually ashamed of.

PART THREE

COASTAL OPERATIONS

'On 16 August we slipped our buoy. It was a stirring sight to see the Fleet going out, all the destroyers first, then the battleships, then us.'

LIEUTENANT GEORGE BLUNDELL, *HMS Kent*

Coastal Operations

The naval war in the Mediterranean proper must necessarily lie outside
the scope of this book, although, however, this part will aim to show
something of the Royal Navy's contribution to the ground fighting in the
desert. The British naval presence in the Mediterranean was made
possible by its bases in Gibraltar, Malta and Alexandria, where the bulk
of the Fleet was stationed. Their defence was a major strategic consideration in British planning during the campaigns in the Middle East
and North Africa.

In the Desert War the Navy operated on the right flank of the British
Army, protecting it from attack by the Axis while pushing on ahead to
attack the enemy's 'left flank'. In addition, the Royal Navy was able to
bring up supplies where needed, making possible the existence of
besieged outposts like Tobruk. The determination with which the Royal
Navy conducted its supporting role was in the finest tradition of the
Senior Service but it had its price: heavy losses to German submarines
and Axis aircraft.

The bombardment of Bardia
and Fort Capuzzo by the
Royal Navy: *Warspite* looses off
her powerful 15-inch guns
(foreground) while directly
behind her *Kent* fires a salvo of
8-inch shells. (E.557E)

HMS *Kent*, a County-class cruiser, was despatched to the Mediterranean on the outset of hostilities with Italy. As the flagship of the 7th Cruiser Squadron under Admiral Renouf, the *Kent* was involved in a number of duties in the eastern Mediterranean. George Blundell was successively torpedo officer, first lieutenant and executive officer aboard the ship. An energetic and conscientious officer, Blundell was not overly impressed by the performance of many of his superiors and recorded their failings in his diary. The *Kent* saw action on 17 August 1940 as part of a force despatched to harry Italian positions around Bardia. Blundell left this record of the Navy considerably at sea:

On 16 August we slipped our buoy. It was a stirring sight to see the Fleet going out, all the destroyers first, then the battleships, then us. We are proceeding in line ahead: *Warspite*, *Malaya*, *Ramillies* and ourselves with a destroyer screen.

There was a wonderful sunrise the next morning and we started to bombard at 07.00 sharp. By this time we could see the column of smoke the Army were making for us but unfortunately the wind blew it flat. *Warspite* firing her fifteen-inch bricks was a grand sight. We fired about ten rounds before we started to 'fire for effect'. You could see our shell bursting on the brow of the hill and sending up clouds of dust. Our forward turrets were firing on almost their furthest aft bearing and the Bridge was dreadful. I went and stood outside the D/F [Direction Finding] office and it felt as if my teeth had been knocked out of my head and my skull cracked. We saw three Gladiators shadowing and protecting our Walrus [spotting aircraft]. It reported that both *Warspite* and ourselves had got on to the targets but that there was no sign of life. The

HMS *Ramillies* sets out into the Mediterranean. Although designed as an ocean-going battleship, the heavy gun armament of ships like *Ramillies* was invaluable in shore-bombardment roles. (A.2383)

C-in-C then ordered the cease fire and we had fired all but six of our hundred rounds.

The Fleet then joined up and we made for home along the coast, the idea being to get bombed and act as a bait so that our own fighters could come out in waves from Alex and shoot down their bombers. It was a perfect day for them with about 50 per cent cloud at ten to fifteen thousand feet. Nothing happened until later in the morning when we heard another ship firing. We soon saw enormous columns of splashes on our port quarter, about a mile away, as one flight of bombers dropped their stuff, while we opened fire on some planes that came out of the clouds.

It really was most exciting, I've never been to any circus which I enjoyed so much. The Captain was terrific in his battle bowler. I don't believe he saw an aircraft from start to finish but he shouted 'Alarm!' 'Open fire!' 'Open fire, dammit!' 'Get on with it!' I'm afraid we fired mostly for the sake of firing. Every time the ADO [Air Defence Officer] saw a target, and opened fire, which the Captain hadn't given the order for, the Captain shouted 'What the hell's the matter, what's going on, where are they?' and promptly pressed the cease-fire gong, generally the eight-inch one. Altogether we opened fire about seven times and fired about ninety-three rounds of four-inch. In one case the aircraft was going in the opposite direction to our shots. In another case we fired at our own aircraft and got nearer than any other time.

The most exciting and awe-inspiring incident was when one of our fighters chased four Eyeties down our port side at a good height. Shortly afterwards we witnessed three planes go down. Two were like great flaming rockets hurtling into the sea. They came down great red glows with a vast tail of black smoke and smashed themselves into the sea – a terrible sight. The third was far away but seemed to just drop into the sea with a terrific splash and we saw the pilot bale out in his parachute. I hope the poor fellow was saved. Nothing more happened after that and we went back to ordinary AA Defence.

Once the British invasion of Libya was under way in January 1941 the Navy was called upon to provide logistic backup. Lieutenant-Commander J. B. Lamb's ship was in dry dock following a torpedo attack off Crete and 'at a loose end' he was involved in helping the Army:

Combined operations was then little more than a definition in a text book and the sight of a sailor in khaki was still a strange one. News of the Western Desert Force's spectacular offensive thrilled everybody and I was highly elated when I was told that I was to be beach-master at Sidi Barrani where the Army wanted supplies landed and prisoners evacuated. I was only given a few hours' notice and with a small party and a scratch kit I sailed westwards.

The X-lighter, which was full of supplies, was a relic of the First War – the Dardanelles I believe – and her maximum speed was three knots. Eventually the cove was reached but owing to the gently shelving beach and the deep draught of the lighter we could not get close in. Our attempts at overcoming our landing difficulties were encouraged by a large muster of military on the shore, amongst whom was a cinema unit. As I prepared to take the plunge with my trousers rolled up, the camera was trained on me. I felt I was not looking my best so it was perhaps fortunate that all evidence was destroyed a few days later when the film-unit's car received a direct hit.

COASTAL OPERATIONS

Soon a semi-floating gangway was rigged but it proved far from satisfactory, merely providing comic relief by turning over from time to time, tipping some unfortunate off. However, the unloading of the badly needed petrol, provisions and water was got under way in fairly quick time using a chain of some 500 prisoners from the several thousands waiting ashore, with the odd one or two up to their necks in water. The Italians did not seem to mind; most welcomed the work as a relief from boredom.

Feeling that my party should be mobile on land I tried to get a captured truck allocated to me, but without success. The following day I resolved to carry into effect this intention of obtaining motor transport, but this time without asking permission from the military authorities. We found a fine, nearly new, Fiat diesel ten-tonner; its only defect was that it had to be towed to start, a failing common to nearly all captured transport. My leading signalman acquired a motor cycle ostensibly so that he could act as despatch rider. I had almost got hold of a staff car when we received orders to move on to Sollum.

It was just as well we had our own transport, for that provided by the Army was far from adequate. Moreover both the truck and the motor cycle subsequently proved absolutely invaluable, and we even found ourselves performing services for the Army with them. That afternoon we broke camp and at teatime set out in company with an ASC convoy. We hoisted a boat's Ensign at the fore, and our progress could almost be described as triumphal.

Sollum was a scene of utter desolation: of the row of buildings along each

Italian prisoners from the Sollum area assist in the discharge of foodstuffs from British supply ships. A naval officer directs operations from the long boat, while an Australian NCO supervises the prisoners from the shore. (E.1558E)

side of the main street only the mosque was standing whole. There was not a soul in sight. Close to the pier was a rather mean-looking dwelling. Here we hoisted the White Ensign and painted 'Admiralty House' on the door. The work of unloading supplies began almost immediately. Labour was provided by a few prisoners and the remains of a company of Argyll & Sutherland Highlanders who were picqueting the harbour.

At Sollum I was able to appreciate the tremendous task of supplying the Army's needs. Everything imaginable passed through our hands – provisions, equipment, bombs, ammunition and even canteen beer. Latrine paper was the greatest nuisance because the bales invariably broke open and their contents were blown all over the harbour. There was an element of irony in this for, originally, there had been a very marked shortage of this commodity.

Commander Lamb followed the Army along the coast to Tobruk and then to Derna before his recall to Alexandria and a return to proper 'blue-water' naval work. F. B. Coombes had been a sailor in coastal waters around Britain before being sent to the Mediterranean in 1940. Based in Alexandria, Coombes was again used in coastal operations, sometimes behind enemy lines. On one occasion Coombes and a partner were reluctantly set ashore to reconnoitre an Italian position:

From the time that Grainger and I lowered ourselves over the bows in our bathing costumes and waited for the rifle and revolver to be passed to us, everything seemed unreal. There was nothing unreal in the revolver I held over my head, however, as we went up the beach. The fact that the Skipper and the lads were manning the guns behind us was not much comfort, and although we

The crew of a quad-mounted 2-pounder pom-pom watches an aerial attack on another vessel. As the Italian surface fleet was normally confined to its anchorages, the main threat to British ships lay from U-boats and Axis aircraft. (A.2364)

set off at a run, it was not to get at the Eyeties but to get out of their line of fire. The quick trot soon slowed down to a shamble as we found that it was further up the hill than we had thought and we ended up making quick dashes until we reached the brow. Eventually I looked over and nearly passed out. In the dip about sixty feet away was an open lorry with a group of Eyeties sitting round brewing tea.

After dropping back from the crest, it took a lot of whispered conversation to convince ourselves that Father Ritchie [the Skipper] would not let us get away with just telling him what we had seen. Grainger wanted to go for help, but he was not leaving me on my Jack up there; I had no wish to be caught and to end up as Bum Boats crew in the Eyetie Army brothel for the rest of my natural.

From the way the Skipper had used the gun earlier we knew that he wanted blood – ours if we let him down – so after a lot of hurried sorting out we decided that we had to split up and come at them from both ends of the dune. Finding a nice big handy rock to hide behind, but still able to see their heads as they sat near each other rattling away and smoking ticklers, I waited and waited for Grainger to fire first shot, according to our plan. Then I saw one of them starting to get up.

Knowing that if he turned round he would see me, I jumped up and put one of my rounds over him or at least in his direction. There was a crash and it went through the lorry windscreen, which perhaps helped to put the wind up them because when I opened my eyes they were all sat down and, better still, had their hands in the air. I don't know who was nearest a wet fart, me or the Eyeties, but we could not have been as windy as Grainger who appeared round the other end of the dune, still on his belly, trying to crawl. After calling Grainger a word which made one of the Eyeties smile I felt a lot braver, enough so to let me go to the one who still had a small revolver in his holster and take it from him. When we counted them, seven soldiers and one officer, I realized that I would have had second thoughts if I had known that there were so many. I quickly told Grainger to prod them together and get them moving back to the boat.

I felt as pleased as a dog with two tails as we herded our prisoners to the boat, one of us on either quarter and just behind them, till we saw Jock Robertson had the Lewis trained on them and us. It's doubtful if Jock could hit them or us, but it's not a nice feeling to be in his line of fire. Worse was to come as we moved the prisoners to the water's edge. Frank Monks was told to put the Coston gun line ashore. Luckily the twitch made at the sound of the shot jerked my head on one side – the rod just missed my ear, although the line put a burn in my shoulder. With the help of a rope we hauled ashore, the soldiers were soon aboard but the officer refused to go. I put a round in the sand between his feet. It made everybody jump but the Eyetie went the highest, as the bullet must have flown high and put a red-hot groove under his lower left duster. He set off like a good 'un and with a hop, skip and jump he was aboard and hardly got his feet wet.

The siege of Tobruk in 1941 was a testing time for the Navy. In order for the garrison to survive, the Navy had to make regular night dashes along the coast, delivering reinforcements, ammunition and provisions while taking off the wounded. Axis air supremacy over Tobruk meant that the convoy runs had to be conducted during the few days each

A light anti-aircraft gun is
made ready for action on a
ship acting as an escort for a
Tobruk convoy, 20 August
1941. (E.4977)

month when there was little or no moonlight. Even then there was no guarantee of a safe passage. Edward Ward accompanied one such convoy on 12 September. After surviving an attack by German torpedo bombers, the British destroyer containing Ward approached Tobruk:

In the dim light of the setting sun I could make out the vague outline of the harbour. We slipped quietly and safely in, threading our way past the wrecks which were dotted about Tobruk harbour. We had no sooner arrived than I heard the dull chug of engines and then we saw the black shape of lighters approaching. Some were filled with men, others were empty to bring off new troops and stores. The Captain shouted his orders from the bridge and the lighters pulled alongside in their allotted places.

Everything was quiet and still and it looked as though we were going to have an easy time of it. But just as the first lot of men had begun to come aboard, the whole sky was lit up by parachute flares. The visiting team had arrived. The shore ack-ack batteries began to open up with everything they had, the whole district ablaze with the flashes of heavy guns. The sky was pin-pointed with balls of flame from the exploding shells, festooned with the tracers from the light ack-ack. Out in the harbour we kept quiet. If we'd started shooting it would only have given us away. Though it seemed to me that our position must have been only too plain with the whole place illuminated by parachute flares which the enemy planes were dropping.

A scene from a Tobruk convoy: with foodstuffs piled on the decks a fast destroyer prepares to run the gauntlet of fire that inevitably accompanied a Tobruk run. (E.6195)

The Captain gave his orders for embarking and disembarking as if nothing was happening. One lot of men came aboard as another lot got off. The ship's crew worked feverishly to get the stores unloaded while planes droned above us, bombs crumped down around the harbour and ack-ack shells burst overhead sending their fragments hissing into the water all round. As the last flares flickered out and the planes turned back we completed our job. Then having done a great deal in a short time we left and made for home.

Out at sea the major danger lay from aerial attack. HMS *Kent* had been ordered to bombard Italian positions around Sollum. George Blundell writes how this normally routine mission turned into a nightmare. His account graphically illustrates the special horrors of a modern sea action while bringing out the human dimension – how some men are overwhelmed by the calamity and rendered useless while others rise to the occasion:

We went to Action Stations. Gun flashes and starshell were seen on our port bow. Then I heard a 'pop' just like one of the exhaust valves momentarily lifting, and then what sounded like steam escaping from an exhaust pipe and suddenly realized it wasn't steam but bombs dropping. They fell to port. We were then firing hard at aircraft and I remember distinctly thinking we'd got a direct hit on one, but it may have been only a shell bursting. Then we had a low torpedo-bomber attack on our starboard beam. I saw the splashes, enormous

HMS *Kent* in port after a two-year cruise in Chinese waters, just before her despatch to the Mediterranean. Launched in 1927 *Kent* was a County-class heavy cruiser with a full-load displacement of 14,000 tons, a maximum speed of 32 knots, a complement of 660 men and a main armament of eight 8-inch guns. Considered to be a good compromise between the conflicting demands of armour, speed and armament the ships of the County class had high standards of durability and endurance and were used extensively as convoy escorts. (A.2561)

ones, as torpedoes were dropped. Shortly afterwards there was a tremendous blow aft. The whole ship reeled, then suddenly went dead, and we could feel on the Bridge as if her tail had dropped, a sort of bending, dragging feeling. The ship wouldn't steer.

All I heard 'Skips' saying was 'CBs', 'CBs' [Confidential Books – the code books which were to be destroyed if the ship was in danger of sinking or capture] and sort of turning round and round on the Bridge and groping around. We were then machine-gunned by aircraft that came in from ahead. I didn't realize what it was at first except that there were loud cracks just like one hears when standing in rifle butts, whilst red worms seemed to fly all around us. At first I thought they were sparks from the funnel. It was too fascinating to be in the least frightening, but when I realized they were bullets, I knelt down to present a smaller target. With the steering gone and the ship stopped it felt exactly like being a man surrounded by assassins with his hands tied behind his back.

I realized that the hit, being aft, had probably put both the after electrical breaker rooms out of action and that emergency cables would have to be run to get power back on to the steering motors, so I asked permission to leave the Bridge to deal with the situation. To my shame I first nipped into my cabin and put my tin containing cine camera and money in a safer place up a deck as it seemed the ship was settling aft. Then I went into the wardroom (WR) flat and saw that the Commander was pretty squiffy. I told someone – it was quite dark so people could only be distinguished by torchlight – to keep an eye on him and sit him down in the wardroom. He looked like a child.

The whole of the after part of the ship was in darkness and silent as the grave as all electric supply had failed. I went to see if emergency cables were being run and yard arm groups supplied. I found some emergency cables hanging down the after engine room hatch and there was a hell of a heat coming up, so I knew that all engine room fans were off. I went down and found the temperature just bearable on the bed plates. I then got hold of EA [Electrical Artificer] Machin to come down with me into the engine room to connect up some breakers, but the heat coming up the hatch was so intense he didn't want to go, so I had to force him down in front of me. I am sure he felt he was going to his death.

I saw the whole WR flat filling with smoke and fumes, obviously coming from aft, so I put on my gas mask. I couldn't see a thing because the eyepieces clouded over and I staggered through an open bulkhead door into the half deck. I couldn't see an inch, not even with my wonderful American torch. There was obviously a big fire raging inside as I could see a glow and it was damned hot. I began to feel a bit chokey and sleepy and sat down inside the flat. I realized that the gas mask was pretty well useless. I felt I could sleep for ever and I remember taking a pull at myself and saying internally, 'No, George Blundell, you're not going to die yet.' So I heaved myself back up and recovered my breath.

I've no idea whether the Commander was in there by this time. Anyhow, I shouted to the four corners of the flat that the bulkhead doors were not to be opened again. Actually, I believe they were, and that it was the Commander who, in a fuddled state, had gone in again to his inevitable death. His body was found outside the 2nd staff office door (where I nearly collapsed) so the poor man didn't get far. It was terrible inside. Then I went up on to the quarterdeck to find a way for the cables to the steering motors in the steering flat. The ship was still being raked by bullets from aircraft and guns seemed to be firing at us from the shore.

I nipped down into the Admiral's dining cabin through the skylight and remember a stoker saying something about spoiling the Admiral's chair covers. I tried to get through the after door but the dogs [catches] had been taken off, so I went to the pantry hatch, but its clips were on the other side. So I was done this way and climbed up on to the quarterdeck again. There I met Chief ERA [Engine Room Artificer] Stephens and said 'How the hell can I get down to the steering motors?' (In fact all normal access to the steering compartment had been blown away by the underwater explosion.) He said 'There's a scuttle [porthole] open down there,' pointing over the side. We got a rope and down we went, myself and Stephens. I found out afterwards that Stephens had already been down and brought back Leading Stoker Johnson, the tiller flat watchkeeper. The ship had settled by the stern so that the sea was only an inch or two below the scuttle rim and I got jambed going in by my gas mask. Inside it was dark as hell and filled with fumes.

As I stepped through the cabin door I squelched on something flabby and in the torchlight saw it was the body of Petty Officer Masters (he died of heart failure). I remember thinking 'That's the first dead man I've ever seen,' and feeling relieved that it didn't seem at all unnatural. After this we worked for about three hours down in the steering flat nearly submerged, getting down lighting and equipment and working the emergency hand pump to supply power. I went up and down about three times making various arrangements and keeping the Bridge informed. The engineers were very slow in getting anybody or anything there. (I learnt years later that the engineer commander, who had newly joined the ship, was an alcoholic and had hidden himself away, and that the senior engineer and many of the engine room staff had passed out due to the heat leaving them out of action for some time.)

We had got a tow off *Nubian* [a destroyer escort]. At first it was impossible to proceed because the rudder was over to starboard and both starboard propellors were out of action, so all we could do was go round in circles. Preparations were made in case we had to abandon ship. At about 0500 everybody had breakfast, and later we were terribly relieved to see [the aircraft carrier] *Illustrious*. Almost the whole Fleet seemed to come out to escort us in. The fire aft was too bad for us to open up and get the bodies out. We put steam on the compartment to damp it out.

There was a nasty swell in the morning as four tugs came out from Alex. The ship was out of control on several occasions and at one time we had to go 160 revs astern starboard and this started the after engine room bulkhead leaking. We berthed near the floating dock and opened up the ship. There were some grim sights. The half deck and the warrant officers' flat looked just like the end of the world. Filled with haze, a dim light coming through the hatches, a terrible stink of dead men and oil fuel, bodies hanging over pipes and trunks or huddled in a shapeless heap, debris, dirt, twisted metal, fittings and cabin furniture flung everywhere.

Once in dock Blundell was appointed Executive Officer. His first task was to cut free the remaining bodies from the crippled ship. Blundell was congratulated for his work in getting HMS *Kent* under way in the most difficult circumstances – an example of how a well-trained and resolute officer could dramatically affect circumstances.

PART FOUR

DEFEAT IN THE DESERT

'We were looking down with our squadron of tanks into a wadi and there as far as the eye could see was the Africa Korps all lined up. We started shelling them – plenty of trucks went up – but there wasn't a great deal we could do to stop them. We had a Stuka attack and our colonel was killed'.

HAROLD FITZJOHN, *22nd Armoured Brigade*

Gazala and the Great Retreat

The Axis reconquest of Cyrenaica had come to a halt against the British line stretching from Gazala on the coast down to the outpost of Bir Hakeim in the south. From early February to mid May 1942 there was a lull in the fighting as both sides built up their strength for the next round of battle.

The Eighth Army under General Neil Ritchie was divided into two corps. As had been the case in the Crusader battles of the previous year, XXX Corps (Lieutenant-General Willoughby Norrie), with 1st and 7th Armoured Divisions, had most of the armour while XIII Corps, (Lieutenant-General W. H. E. Gott) contained the bulk of the infantry. The infantry divisions were distributed along the defensive line which consisted of a series of boxes, protected by barbed wire and minefields and capable of holding a brigade group. While affording the infantry a

Lieutenant-General Neil
Ritchie (centre, in battledress
blouse) consults his two corps
commanders Norrie (left) and
Gott as the crisis deepens, 31
May 1942. Norrie and Gott
were senior to Ritchie and
relations between army and
corps commanders were
poor, especially as Norrie and
Gott felt their experience in
the field counted for more
than Ritchie's time as
Auchinleck's Deputy Chief of
Staff. (E.12633)

94

degree of protection from enemy armour, the box system effectively locked them up, away from the main battle (*see* Boxes and Jock Columns, page 116). The British armour was dispersed evenly behind the line.

Reinforced from Europe (along with the windfall provided by captured British supplies at Benghazi), Rommel prepared to resume the offensive, not only to complete the capture of Cyrenaica but to press on towards the prizes of Cairo, Alexandria and the Suez Canal. Rommel's plan was simple and direct, relying on speed and aggression to achieve success. Group Cruewell, comprising Italian infantry with German support, would attack the British line to pin down the defenders while Rommel would lead the Axis armoured divisions in a wide sweep to the south of Bir Hakeim. Outflanking the British defensive line the Axis tanks would then take on the British armoured units and cut off the bulk of the Eighth Army from its supply lines to the east.

On the afternoon of 26 May, Group Cruewell began its assault, and under cover of darkness the German and Italian armoured formations began their outflanking movement. Major John Hackett (later to achieve fame at Arnhem) was the commander of a squadron of M3 Stuart light tanks in the 8th King's Royal Irish Hussars. On the morning of 27 May he was ordered forward to investigate reports of enemy activity south of the Bir Hakeim box:

M3 Stuart light tanks are put through their paces by the 8th King's Royal Irish Hussars. Their thin armour and high-octane petrol engines made them highly vulnerable to enemy fire – as Major John Hackett was to experience on the opening day of Gazala. (E.5065)

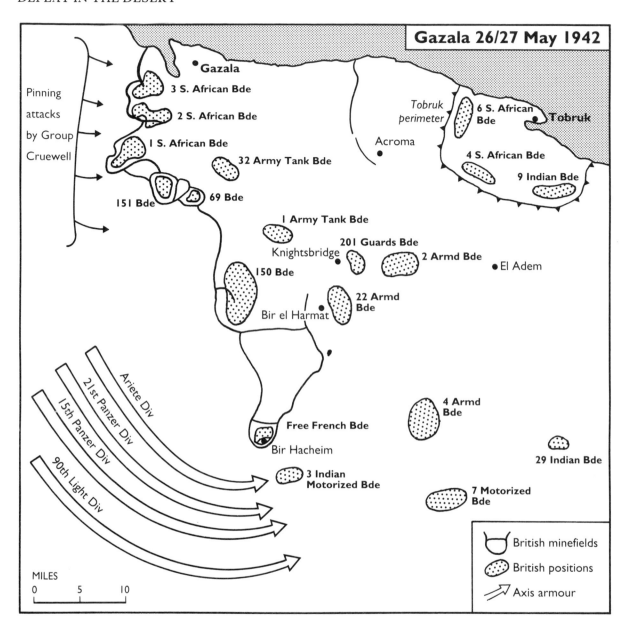

Gazala 26/27 May 1942

Pinning attacks by Group Cruewell

Gazala
3 S. African Bde
2 S. African Bde
1 S. African Bde
32 Army Tank Bde
151 Bde
69 Bde

Tobruk perimeter
Acroma

6 S. African Bde
Tobruk
4 S. African Bde
9 Indian Bde

1 Army Tank Bde
Knightsbridge
201 Guards Bde
2 Armd Bde
El Adem
150 Bde
22 Armd Bde
Bir el Harmat

Ariete Div
21st Panzer Div
15th Panzer Div
90th Light Div

Free French Bde
Bir Hacheim
3 Indian Motorized Bde

4 Armd Bde
29 Indian Bde
7 Motorized Bde

MILES
0   5   10

British minefields
British positions
Axis armour

I got C Squadron on the move very quickly – they were a very handy lot. We went up a slope in this typically undulating desert country, and as I reached the top of this rise the commanding officer said to me over the radio: 'Report when you first see them.' I came over the top and there in front of me was the whole bloody German army, as far as I could see – coming my way.

I replied to the colonel's transmission: 'I'm engaging them. Out.' I put up a black flag to say 'Attack!' – in those days wireless was not too reliable – and like a mug forgot to take it down again. And any tank flying a flag is of course a control element and attracts fire, so I attracted all the fire there was. I suppose my tank was the first in the Eighth Army to be knocked out that day, which was about three minutes after putting up the black flag.

Despite being 'quite badly burnt' in his desperate attempt to delay the Afrika Korps's progress, Hackett managed to get back to his regiment and was eventually evacuated to hospital. Further north, Harold Fitzjohn, in the 22nd Armoured Brigade, was similarly surprised by the sudden arrival of the German armour:

We were looking down with our squadron of tanks into a wadi and there as far as the eye could see was the Afrika Korps all lined up. We started shelling them – plenty of trucks went up – but there wasn't a great deal we could do to stop them. We had a Stuka attack and our colonel was killed.

The South Notts Hussars provided artillery support for the 22nd Armoured Brigade and was soon in the thick of the action. When the Germans had been sighted sweeping round Bir Hakeim, two armoured cars were sent forward to reconnoitre the advance. The first contained the battery commander, Major Garry Birkin, and the second, his brother Captain Ivor Birkin, along with Harold Harper, an NCO in the Regiment:

We had only gone six or seven hundred yards when we heard a garbled message from the commander's radio which immediately told us something was wrong. Captain Birkin jumped out and dashed across to the armoured car, and I followed him. I've never seen anything quite like it in my life. Major Birkin lay flat on the floor, obviously dead. I went to the back and opened up the doors of the armoured car. Apparently an armour-piercing shell had gone clean through the middle of the battery commander as he was standing in the turret and then chopped off the heads of the two radio operators. All you could see was the two lads, their hands still holding their mouthpieces – although their heads had rolled off onto the floor. The third radio operator, who had sent the message, jumped down from the armoured car and raced off.

The sequence of disasters for the gunners was to continue. While Ivor Birkin remained at the scene of destruction by the knocked out armoured car, Harper went back to his vehicle. Then, however, he decided:

I must go back and pick up Captain Birkin, who was in a very distraught state, having seen his brother killed. I put my hand on the driver, who had by that time pulled down all the shutters and was driving blind. We had practised for weeks, whereby I would put down a certain pressure on either the left or right shoulder and according to the amount of pressure, the driver turned the wheel to a varying degree.

In the turmoil I put too much pressure on the lad's shoulder and he turned sharply, and just out of a cloud of dust came a Grant tank of the Royal Gloucester Hussars. We hit it head on and literally bounced back five or six yards. The next thing we saw was the engine on fire. We all had to jump out of the thing. In the meantime we found we had accidentally run over the laddie who had been the third radio operator in Major Birkin's crew. We'd run over and broken his leg, so we had to drag him with us. The four of us, plus the lad, went over to Captain Birkin. And there we were, stranded.

We then jumped on the back of a passing tank of the CLY [County of London Yeomanry] and lay flat on it. The tank commander had no idea we

Above: A British Grant tank moves past a knocked out Axis tank during the Gazala fighting, 6 June 1942. The Grant was an unusual design, utilizing a 37mm gun in the turret and a 75mm main gun mounted in the hull. (E.12920)

were there and kept on firing. We had to keep dodging as best we could when the turret and barrel kept swinging round. One of the chaps fell off and we thought he'd been crushed to death, though I found out later that he lived. Most of us received wounds of some sort from the German shelling. I'd crushed my ribs when we collided with the Grant tank and later I got some shrapnel in my left knee. I wasn't aware of this at the time, there was too much happening.

How we didn't get thrown off the tank was a miracle – you slithered around and hoped for the best. The gun was firing about six inches from my ear. We kept hammering away at the turret and eventually the officer opened the flap and saw what was happening. He said he couldn't do much for us but took us back to his wagon lines for treatment, and then went back into the action.

A few hours later while Harper was having his wounds attended to at the Field Dressing Station, they were overrun by a German panzer unit. The Germans allowed the medical staff to continue their work. Suddenly a light plane landed by the dressing station to reveal a high-ranking German officer whom Harper recognized as General Erwin Rommel: 'At the height of the battle he took time to say that everything possible would be done to make the British prisoners comfortable, and that he was sorry they couldn't get any food through as yet but they would try. I couldn't fail but be impressed by him.'

Right: The charismatic Afrika Korps commander, Erwin Rommel, gives orders to one of his officers. (HU.16766)

Rommel's inspired leadership contrasted favourably with the lacklustre performance shown in the British camp. The Eighth Army's reaction to the German armoured attack had been slow and unco-ordinated. Relations between Ritchie and his two corps commanders were not good and there was general disagreement as to what the correct British response should be. At corps and divisional level few attempts were made by formations to operate in conjunction with each other, so that piecemeal British counter attacks were defeated in detail by the Afrika Korps. The absence of urgency displayed by the British command is illustrated in the following transcript. Lieutenant D. F. Parry was stationed with his mobile repair workshop on the south of the British position and became aware of the German advance on the morning of the 27th:

It was about 0800 hours when, failing to raise my regimental headquarters, I ordered my wireless operator to search adjacent bands in case the wavelengths had been changed without our knowledge. Almost immediately we picked up a transmission 'in clear', a little unusual as all messages were passed in code prior to a battle. Clear and concise, it was like a BBC outside broadcast; even after thirty years the conversation is as sharp today as it was in 1942. The officer, obviously well south, was sending a message to XXX Corps HQ at El Adem.

OFFICER: There is a cloud of dust to the south; it has the appearance of a military formation.

REPLY FROM XXX CORPS: There are no, repeat no, troops to your south. However, 7th Armoured Division is positioned to the west.

OFFICER: The cloud of dust is growing larger. It is undoubtedly a military formation.

REPLY (*slightly irritable*): We repeat, there are no, repeat no, troops to your south.

OFFICER: Through the haze I can now identify tanks, difficult to identify but possibly German Mark IVs.

REPLY: We repeat, there are no troops, repeat no troops, to your south.

OFFICER: I can now positively identify German Mark IV tanks together with motorized infantry; it appears to be a large German force.

REPLY (*irritably*): We repeat no, repeat no, forces in your vicinity.

OFFICER: I am counting Mark IVs – one, two, three, four, five, six, seven – there is no doubt, repeat no doubt, that this is a large German force. Mark IVs number over thirty, and there are also Mark IIIs and a large number of motorized infantry. This could be, I repeat, this could be the Afrika Korps moving at a speed of approximately 30 miles per hour towards El Adem.

REPLY (*with air of resignation*): There are no forces in your area.

OFFICER: I have been spotted by the enemy and am under fire. (In the background one could hear the ominous sound of exploding shells. However, our intrepid broadcaster's tone did not change one iota from start to finish.) I repeat, it is a large enemy formation and probably the Afrika Korps moving fast northwards.

REPLY (*very bored*): There are no enemy forces in your area.

OFFICER: It is undoubtedly the Afrika Korps moving at speed towards El Adem. I am under . . .

Then there was silence.

Mounting a 5cm main gun, a PzKpfw III of the Afrika Korps rumbles across the desert battlefield, June 1942. Along with the more heavily armed Mark IV tank (7.5cm gun) the Mark III was the mainstay of the German panzer divisions in North Africa. (MH.5852)

Despite the setbacks suffered by the British on the first day of fighting, the battle was not necessarily lost. Rommel had driven his armoured forces deep behind the British line but Eighth Army morale held firm and, although poorly planned, British counter-attacks were beginning to wear down the panzers' offensive capability. After a couple of days of fierce but inconclusive tank combat Rommel's position began to worsen. The British armour had failed to melt away at the first great onslaught while German supplies of ammunition and petrol were on the verge of running perilously low.

Rommel had hoped to force a supply route through the centre of the British line but he had underestimated the depth of the minefields and was unaware of the presence of the 150 Brigade box astride his proposed route. If this lifeline was to be established then 150 Brigade would have to be eliminated with the greatest rapidity. Rommel ordered his divisions to withdraw into a defensive position on the edge of the minefields while the 150 Brigade box was destroyed.

The full weight of the Afrika Korps was thrown against the hapless 150 Brigade. For nearly seventy-two hours three battalions of infantry supported by the brigade artillery and engineers plus a squadron of tanks weathered the German storm. Sheer weight of numbers and shortage of ammunition told against the defenders and on 1 June, the position was taken. Rommel was deeply impressed by the British stand

and later wrote that his troops, 'had met the toughest resistance imaginable. The defence was conducted with marked skill, and as usual the British fought to the end.' A. H. G. Dobson was the Royal Engineer brigade major and he describes the final stage of the struggle:

They mopped up 150 Brigade. All the guns had been lost or were out of ammunition and the few tanks we had were all out of action. It was just the foot soldier sitting in a hole in the ground with a Bren gun and he hadn't really much hope by that stage. I remember the sapper commander on the phone saying 'I can see the tanks coming now,' and by the time they were 50 yards away he said, 'I don't think I shall be telephoning much more.' That was the end of his particular unit, and this went on all the way round.

Eventually the Brigade commander [Brigadier C. W. Haydon, killed shortly afterwards in the last German attack] announced that as far as 150 Brigade was concerned the war was over and it really became *sauve qui peut* [every man for himself]. I went off with four or five others in a scout car. We hoped we might manage to drive through the minefield. We got a long way before there was the usual explosion and the wheel was blown off. We just sat there hoping we hadn't been seen, but we had and we were shelled – it was very unpleasant. That night we set off to walk back towards (we hoped) our lines, but after a long night's walking we ran into a German LOC [Lines of Communication] unit who, praise them, were very good to us.

The destruction of 150 Brigade box allowed the free passage of supplies to the Germans in their defensive perimeter – called the Cauldron – who could then go on to the offensive. Instead, Rommel waited for the British tanks to throw themselves on his carefully sited anti-tank screen. And this the British obligingly did. Although Ritchie had had several days to plan and execute a thorough counter-attack nothing was done. A strange combination of indecision and complacency ruled the Eighth Army's decision-making process. Indeed, Ritchie thought he had the battle virtually won when the Germans had withdrawn into the Cauldron. But the prompt and concerted attack that might have beaten the Germans never came.

Undoubtedly, there was great confusion in the British camp which made swift, decisive action difficult. The HQ of the 7th Armoured Division had been overrun and its commander, Major-General Frank Messervy, captured. John Hackett observed the incident:

Messervy had been put in the bag. I actually saw it happen. He was visiting a corps and they were being surrounded by German armour. But he escaped – great pity! Messervy was an old-style Indian cavalry general who didn't know anything about armour. The Germans had him as a prisoner and – so the story went – they were all lined up and there was Messervy who had taken off his medal ribbons and badges of rank. A German officer came up to him and said, 'My God, they must be hard pressed over on your side to be sending up poor old buggers like you!'

In the confusion of battle Messervy and most of his staff managed to give the captors the slip. Hackett continues the story:

Meanwhile Lumsden [Major-General Herbert Lumsden, commanding 1st

Armoured Division] was attempting to combine his division with the remnants of 7th Armoured Division to make a concentrated counter-attack against Rommel, who was then in trouble on the British minefields. On his arrival within British lines Messervy forbade the inclusion of his forces in the attack until the arrival of reinforcements. A golden opportunity missed. When Herbert Lumsden was given this message and saw the counter-attack cancelled he took off his hat and threw it on the ground – it was a most expressive gesture. He knew it was our last chance of stopping Rommel.

As Rommel built up his strength in the Cauldron during the first few days of June, so the Eighth Army slowly prepared its counter-attack. Operation Aberdeen got under way on 5 June and was a complete failure. Not only was Rommel prepared for it, but the attack was badly organized with infantry and armour operating independently of each other. The next two accounts – one infantry, the other armour – reveal the shortcomings of British planning and the heavy price paid by the men who had to carry out the orders at the sharp end. Richard Bromley-Gardener's battalion of Highland Light Infantry formed part of the 10th Indian Infantry Brigade which attacked the German positions in the Cauldron from the east:

My carrier platoon was sent off with a section to each of the two leading infantry companies while I was kept back by the colonel with the remaining half-dozen

After his escape from German captivity Major-General Frank Messervy is congratulated by one of his officers from the 7th Armoured Division. (E.12872)

Lorry-borne troops and Bren carriers of the Highland Light Infantry move up to take part in Operation Aberdeen, the ill-fated British attack on the Cauldron. (E.13122)

carriers. As it got lighter so it appeared that one company did reach its objective. The other didn't – it was bogged down and the colonel sent me across with the remainder of the carrier platoon, taking the Bren guns with us to give extra firepower.

I remember going across the desert at high speed with the other six carriers behind me. Very often the commander in each carrier would be sitting up alongside the driver, who was down below the level of the wall armour, while the chap at the back would be sitting up manning a Bren gun. I had dropped down to look at my map because I wasn't absolutely sure if we were in the right spot when there was a great bang, like having a puncture in a car.

The carrier came to a grinding halt and I found myself covered with mess. The driver seemed to be unconscious or dead. I jumped out of the carrier and found that it was right off its tracks on one side. My driver, Murray, was not dead but knocked out, and when I went round the back there was no sign of the other chap, except half a torso. The shell had hit the side of the carrier and exploded, blowing off everything that was poking out above the top: the Bren gun and all the top hamper – and all the top half of this wretched gunner. The carrier was finished and we were stuck in the desert.

I tried to wave down one of the other carriers which were screaming past us; the last one fortunately did see we were in trouble and came over. Murray was then capable of pulling himself out of the carrier and just as he did so the thing caught on fire. We grabbed our map cases and weapons, transferred to this other carrier and off we went to join the company which was then under pretty heavy fire. Eventually we were pinned down – nothing had happened – and I was called back to battalion headquarters.

The 22nd Armoured Brigade mounted an attack on Sidra Ridge, which marked the northern edge of the Cauldron. Harold Fitzjohn was driving a Matilda tank:

We advanced at first light under a smoke screen and when we got through the

The maelstrom of fire that
was the battle of the Cauldron
– seen from British positions
about a mile distant. In such
open terrain the British
assault stood little chance
against the Germans'
carefully sited anti-tank
screen. (E.13100)

smoke we found ourselves in the middle of a minefield which no one knew was there. Sited all along the front were dug-in 88mm guns which started potting off our tanks, like in a shooting gallery. As we tried to get past the minefield the best part of the 21st Panzer Division came round our right flank and started belting away at us.

We didn't know what was happening. The next tank to me was our troop leader, Lieutenant Coulton. He got his head blown off but I couldn't tell you how it happened. You're too busy looking after yourself – you only see a small piece of the battlefield.

The panzers came on; we heard their 75mm and 50mm shells banging into our right-hand side. The first shell that hit us showered me with aluminium paint from the inside of the tank. Then a shot came and smashed my periscope but the shell had twisted the casing around it and I couldn't pull the broken prism out. I was in a horrible position: should I open up and repair the damage or should I wait?

Then we had another big bang and the intercom went dead. Now I was driving blind. It was absolute chaos. Suddenly we were hit in the turret and it jammed – the tank was useless. I was told to turn round and away we came. As we were coming back out I opened up my driver's hatch – as I knew it was comparatively safe – and my heart sank into my boots, for as far as the eye could see were Matildas on fire or knocked out. I passed one and there was our squadron leader laid out on the side of it. When we got back there was a roll call – there were twelve of us out of the seventy that went in.

The failure of Operation Aberdeen was the signal for Rommel to burst out of the Cauldron. On the afternoon of 5 June the tanks of 21st Panzer Division smashed their way through the British, towards the Knightsbridge position, while 15th Panzer Division swung around through Bir el Harmat to the south. The British were now fighting a desperate holding action to prevent the German armour from overwhelming the entire Gazala position. The CO of the 7th RTR, Colonel H. R. B. Foote, was ordered to relieve a regiment which had run out of ammunition while holding open the eastern side of the Knightsbridge position:

My orders were to hold off the German armour so that the Guards Brigade could be withdrawn that night. The main problem was that there were no hull-down positions. The desert here was a flat plain and we were soon suffering a lot of tank casualties, the leading squadron being practically wiped out. In order to hold on I decided to deploy my two remaining squadrons on each side of my headquarters tank with orders to conform to my movements. When the enemy started to get our range I moved our tanks either forwards or backwards a few hundred yards to confuse him. Luckily with the help of a sandstorm and the use of smoke we were able to hold out till dark, but at the end of the engagement we only had seven operational tanks left.

During the battle I noticed that my own tank was not firing. On asking the gunner (my adjutant, Captain McClean) what was the matter, he said he could not close the breach block. On looking outside I was not surprised, as an enemy shell had gone down the barrel of my two-pounder and had splayed it out like the skin of a banana. At the end of the day my crew counted twenty-nine direct hits on my own tank but luckily none had penetrated the thick armour of the Matilda.

Colonel Foote's memoir recounts how his regiment was forced back towards Tobruk and how he was eventually captured by the Germans. What the memoir modestly fails to tell us is that Foote was repeatedly wounded during the battle but continued to lead his regiment, for which he was awarded the Victoria Cross. Sadly, the steadfastness and bravery of the British officers and men were not sufficient to save the Eighth Army.

With the destruction of the British armour virtually complete, Rommel turned directly south to eliminate the Bir Hakeim box. Defended by a brigade of Free French, Bir Hakeim was now vulnerable to German pressure. Bombarded from land and air the French fought on as best they could but running low on supplies their position was becoming untenable. On 10 June the order was given for the French to break out of the box, which with the aid of a diversionary attack by the remnants of XXX Corps was a success, 2700 men out of an original 3600 making their way to safety.

What remained of the British defensive line faced encirclement as Rommel reorganized his tired forces to advance on Tobruk. In the far north, 1st South African Division made good its escape on the night of 13/14 June but for the two brigades of 50th Division their situation was more difficult. 69 Brigade was able to retreat directly eastwards along the coast road but for 151 Brigade the novel solution was proposed that it should advance westwards (ie the 'wrong' way) into the Axis positions before swinging south of Bir Hakeim and back towards Egypt. Newly appointed as commander of D Company, 8th Durham Light Infantry (DLI), Harold Sell was instructed to draw up a breakout plan for the brigade:

It was explained to me that the breakout must be done quickly before the enemy

Foreign Legionnaires of the Free French Brigade based in the Bir Hakeim box make the best of British rations in the period before the German offensive. The French defence of Bir Hakeim was held up as an example of the rejuvenation of French military spirit after the disasters of 1940. (E.8397)

had time to probe our defences in greater strength. I was told I had to make a bridgehead in the Italian line and had to eliminate the German strongpoints. I was given the rough distances to the enemy troops, some photographs, bits of sketches and was given half an hour to think it over. I went back to the meeting and requested no artillery support: without gunfire surprise would be achieved and I might be able to get into the enemy positions without being fired on by their heavy stuff. It would be in the lap of the gods after that. They agreed to my plan and I got my company ready.

While Sell's company started the attack the rest of the 8th DLI would force their way past the Axis lines. They were to be followed by the other two battalions in 151 Brigade, 6th and 9th DLI. W. I. Watson was an officer in the 6th battalion:

We had to take enough food for three days and enough petrol for three hundred miles. The feeling in the box then was pretty grim. Everything not wanted was buried in case the breakout failed and we had to come back. We formed up at dusk and each column was to be led by a South African armoured car and an intelligence section with a compass, plus some sappers in case we had to lift any mines.

As the British waited for the light to fade, Sell's company stealthily lifted the mines directly in front of them. When evening came:

Sand-caked soldiers of the Durham Light Infantry smile for the camera after their desert breakout – an example of the indomitable spirit of the British soldier. (E.13574)

We raced forward as fast as we could. We went in vehicles and almost got to the enemy positions before they realized what had happened. My truck was hit by an anti-tank gun and blown to pieces, but I was lucky as both myself and the driver were all right. Then we went through their dugouts with grenades and Tommy guns and cleared the whole lot out. We overran the Germans with our Marmon Herrington armoured cars; shot up all their machine-guns. They were eliminated, as were the Italians.

We now took up defensive positions on either side of the gap we had made. Then the 8th and 6th battalions went through. There were only isolated attacks from the Italians as our troops got away – the whole lot took an hour. The trouble started afterwards, because Joss Percy [CO of 9th DLI] came to the conclusion, after hearing all the noise of battle, that we'd been destroyed. So he turned his battalion the other way and forced his way back to Tobruk and to Mersa Matruh.

At the time I was having a council of war with my officers, wondering what the hell to do. We didn't know what they were doing and we couldn't reach them on the radio as it had been destroyed by gunfire. We stuck it out until dawn. By that time the Germans had rallied their troops and we were being pretty heavily pounded and suffering casualties. I said to my men, 'That's it, let's get out.' So we broke out into the desert and swept round the old Free French position at Bir Hakeim, being shot up by the Germans. When I got past the minefields I had three armoured cars, myself and two other blokes. That was all, the rest of the company had been wiped out.

W. I Watson provides this account of the breakout by the main body:

Prompt at 8 o'clock the 8th Battalion did their attack and then we started to go through their gap which was the width of the column. As we advanced, the enemy began to realize what was happening and they began shelling us. The truck of the CO went up on a mine killing the driver. This held up my column and we were now being shot at. To add to our difficulties the armoured car in my column also went up on a mine. Somehow we managed to crawl past the armoured car without going up on a mine ourselves.

When we were out I said to my chaps: 'If you stick to my tail, I'll do my best to get you through.' It was a fearfully nasty experience, driving across the German positions along the Trigh Capuzzo. We saw the German bivouacs and camp fires. We drove for 30 miles into the desert and I went on for another five to make sure we were really well clear. By now all sorts of vehicles from other columns were tacking on to me. I remember a great big German three-tonner lorry came bearing down on us in the dark and we were just going to put a shot into it when we heard a lot of Geordie voices inside – they were from the 8th Battalion and had captured it when making their escape.

Although 151 Brigade lost most of their vehicles and heavy weapons, over 90 per cent of the men eventually managed to get back to British lines. It was a minor epic of the Desert War but only a small compensation for the tragedy about to unfold – the fall of Tobruk.

The Eighth Army had been out-generalled and out-fought in three weeks of intense fighting. On 16 June the British began to fall back towards the Egyptian frontier. This retreat ensured that Tobruk – containing around 35,000 men and a vast mountain of supplies – would again come under siege. Despite the numbers of troops in Tobruk – a mixed British and South African force under the command of Major-General H. B. Klopper – the situation was very different from that of the previous year when the port had successfully sustained an eight-month siege. The anti-tank defences had largely been dismantled (anti-tank guns were in particularly short supply) and the entire command structure was disorganized as a consequence of the defeat at Gazala.

Rommel wasted no time in this second attempt to secure Tobruk. On 20 June, under the cover of a furious bomber attack, his armoured divisions smashed their way into the south-eastern corner of the perimeter defences. Within hours a breech had been made and Rommel's panzers raced through directly towards Tobruk harbour. Despite a few gallant but isolated stands the defence crumbled almost immediately. By the evening of 21 June all resistance had come to an end. Not only did the fall of Tobruk provide Rommel with nearly 33,000 prisoners and a wealth of supplies, a grateful Führer promoted him to the rank of *Generalfeldmarschall*.

The loss of Tobruk was a disaster for British pride of arms: Churchill called it a disgrace, and rancour over responsibility for the failure was to continue well after the war. Bertram Martin, a signaller in the 67th Medium Regiment, Royal Artillery, based in Tobruk, wrote about his capture:

We were Stuka'd and bombed continually for two or three days prior to the fall of Tobruk. I had very mixed feelings at the time; it came as a relief because of the incessant bombing and shelling but I also thought we could have held out longer, like our predecessors did a year previously. However, I didn't think certain people or sections of the Army did enough to defend Tobruk.'

Groups of men tried to escape the German net around Tobruk but only the most resolute and lucky managed to slip through. Amongst these was Captain Owen Bird:

I was medical officer to one of the South African battalions in Tobruk. My Regimental Aid Post was in a cave which formed an excellent shelter and I was able to carry on my work at the height of the bombing and shelling. We knew there had been a breakthrough when, from the entrance to the cave, we saw enemy tanks making their way into the centre of town. All that night [20/21 June] we heard them trundling in. We spent a restless night expecting to be confronted by masses of Jerries at any moment. Early the next morning the commanding officer said that it was all over and would we like to make a bid to get away.

We set off in my desert buggy and had to pass through a patrol gap on the minefield where the sappers had hastily lifted the mines. We got through safely but the ambulance just behind us was blown up. Fortunately nobody was hurt but the ambulance lay across the track and was causing congestion for the vehicles behind, which soon brought down heavy shell fire. We tried dragging the ambulance out of the way but it was firmly in the hole made by the mine blast. All we could do was gingerly lift the mines to the side and make a new track.

I picked up those who had been in the ambulance and with nine men hanging onto my little truck I found an opening, driving through the cordon of enemy units advancing on Tobruk. After a hectic drive of about seventy miles, in which we had to dodge enemy columns and vehicles, we met a patrol from an Indian brigade and realized that we had fooled the Hun and were safe.

A regular soldier in the King's Own Scottish Borderers, F. M. V. Tregear had been appointed as a liaison officer to the South African forces in Tobruk. He describes the German assault and the breakdown of order within the perimeter:

Although probing attacks had been made on the South African position to the west, the main attack was on the south-east flank, with heavy shelling and divebombing by Stukas all along the front held by the Mahrattas [a battalion of

11th Indian Infantry Brigade]. It was impossible to see what was happening owing to the thick dust, smoke and sand clouds thrown up by the shelling and bombing, while the Germans were quick to take advantage of the gaps between the Allied posts. Although the Gurkhas put in a counter-attack this was largely abortive owing to limited visibility and for fear of attacking the already hard-pressed and unhappy Mahrattas. They were also subject to the heavier fire power of the German tanks and infantry, which was increasing every minute.

About midday, HQ of 11th Indian Infantry Brigade was overrun. On learning the news Major-General Klopper is reported to have said: 'My crust is broken, all is lost.' Whatever the truth of this may be, all cohesion fizzed out and the whereabouts of Klopper and his HQ became a matter of conjecture. South African Rear HQ (where I was at the time) was completely in the dark as to the situation and did not know what to do. My task had obviously come to an end. From then on I became a spectator.

I found confusion everywhere. About 6pm the CO of the Pretoria Police Battalion arrived fuming with rage and frustration. He had been organizing his battalion into tank-hunting groups, but had then received an order not to do so. 'Why,' he asked, 'has Tobruk surrendered?' No one could tell him. I found the men of the South African Division itching to fight. In my opinion, if only the men had been allowed to go in, I feel the outcome could well have been different. As it was the South African Division sat tight and did nothing.

The Eighth Army's troubles were still far from over. In the last few weeks it had lost 50,000 men and as it fell back to the Egyptian frontier it was still being harried by the Germans. Rommel had the scent of victory in his nostrils and he pushed his men ruthlessly – one last effort and the Delta would be theirs. By the 23 June the battered Eighth Army had taken up a line by Mersa Matruh.

A view from a German aircraft of the bomber attack on Tobruk which preceded the main assault by German armour on 20 June 1942. The speed and violence of Rommel's offensive completely overwhelmed the defenders of Tobruk. (HU.40248)

The loneliness of command:
General Sir Claude
Auchinleck stands by the
roadside and watches his
troops retreating from Mersa
Matruh, having just assumed
direct command of the Eighth
Army in the face of a series of
defeats by the Afrika Korps.
(E.13881)

Auchlinleck decided that he must take over control of the Army himself and on 25 June Ritchie was discreetly relieved of his command. Realizing the danger faced by the British forces around Matruh, Auchinleck began to order a withdrawal to better positions at Alamein. Rommel struck first, however: large numbers of British troops were trapped in the Matruh fortress and those that got away suffered another mauling at the hands of the Afrika Korps.

Despite the vicissitudes experienced by 151 Brigade at Gazala they were still in the line when the Germans pushed forward from Mersa Matruh. Harold Sell describes an incident prior to the main German attack (in which Sell was captured):

We were all on the escarpment near Mersa Matruh. Enemy patrols were probing around, throwing grenades, with us shooting back at them. That night we were being shot at by German six-wheeled armoured cars. We had just been issued with new six-pounder guns. Nobody knew how to fire them but one of the gun crews decided to stalk an armoured car. They pulled the gun to where they could see the armoured car, opened the breech and focused on the car down the barrel. They quickly put a round in and fired. As it was only 100 yards away they blew it to smithereens.

Even though the Eighth Army had suffered this series of set-backs,

'The General of an Armoured Division Sitting Beside his Tank' by Edward Ardizonne. According to Ardizonne, this was a portrait of the commander of the 10th Armoured Division (Major-General A. R. Gatehouse) and his staff shortly before the breakthrough at Alamein. (LD 2769)

'Troops in the Birka' by Edward Ardizonne. British soldiers are importuned by the local population in the red light district of Cairo. (LD 2529)

'An Eighth Army Brigade Preparing for an Attack, July 1942' by Edward
Copnall. An early morning scene during the First Battle of Alamein.
(LD 5737)

'With the Quartermaster Near Seclin' by Edward Bawden. (LD 201)

'Havildar Kulbir Thapa, 2/3 Gurkha Regiment' by Sir William
Coldstream. (LD 3992)

'25-Pounder Gun and Team in Action on the El Alamein Front' by John Berry. A dynamic action piece of the workhorse of British artillery taking on distant Axis targets at the high watermark of the Desert War. (LD 2788)

'Halfaya Pass' by Jack Chaddock. A column of British Vehicles winds its
way through Halfaya Pass, the Eighth Army's gateway into Libya.
(LD 3403)

'The Advance Continues' by Jack Chaddock. A six-pounder anti-tank gun
travels along the coast road towards El Agheila as part of the follow up
to the Battle of Alamein. (LD 3402)

'The Great Landing' by Anthony Gross. The scene depicts the survivors of an epic voyage from Crete to North Africa during the evacuation of Crete, May–June 1941 (LD 2751)

'The Battle of Egypt, 1942. Bombing up' by Anthony Gross. A Tomahawk is made ready for action. (LD 2734)

discipline and morale held up well during the long march back to Alamein. Certainly there was confusion in many soldiers' minds as to why, yet again, they had been thrown back by the Germans but the will to fight had not been eroded. One commentator called the Eighth Army 'brave but baffled'. Theodore Stephanides made this comment:

What impressed me most was the discipline and order that prevailed everywhere. It was almost impossible to believe that this was a hurried and unexpected retreat. Everybody seemed cheerful and in spite of the numbers and speed of the traffic, I did not see a single collision. Military Police were posted at various points to direct and regulate the traffic and everything proceeded as smoothly as clockwork, rather like a crowd leaving a popular race meeting.

At Alamein Auchinleck made his stand. His formations were seriously depleted but Rommel's forces were short of supplies and nearing the point of exhaustion. The two weary gladiators steeled themselves for one last encounter. The first Axis attack on the Alamein position came on 2 July. Rommel intended to bypass the position as he had done at Gazala and Mersa Matruh but his advance was checked on the Ruweisat ridge. Hoping to outflank the British, the Axis armoured units were forced further south.

Meanwhile, the Eighth Army had been reinforced with the arrival of the 9th Australian Infantry Division, which took up positions around El Alamein. On 10 July, supported by British tanks, the Australians launched a surprise attack towards the slight rise known as Tell el Eisa. Maurice Trigger was in the 2/2nd Machine Gun Battalion when he moved up to the front line:

On the way through we were full of death and glory at the thought of going into action, having a wonderful time hanging on the back of the trucks. Then three trucks in front of us hit a land mine. I remember the yelling and screaming of the fellows after the explosion died down, like dogs yelping. Our death and glory attitude deflated like a bloody airship hit by a bullet; we were seeing what could happen and everyone was quite subdued after that.

The speed of the Australian advance caught the Axis completely by surprise. The Italian Sabratha Division was destroyed and Rommel was forced to divert his armour from the southern front to come to the aid of the beleaguered troops on the coast. Dug in on the Tel el Eisa, the Australians now had to face the weight of the German counter-attack. Brigade major to the 26th Brigade – and one of the planners of the attack on 10 July – Charles Finlay witnessed the German reaction and Allied countermeasures:

At one stage on 12 July they sent the whole of the 90th Light Division into the attack. Brigadier Ramsay, the Commander Royal Artillery of the 9th Division, was given the artillery of the two divisions south of him to go to work on the Germans. They really tore into them. I think they lost twenty-two tanks that afternoon. The Germans always used to attack then, out of the setting sun; it was very hard to see them in the desert. The German tanks had to keep going to avoid the shellfire, whereas the infantry in the personnel carriers were being

A well-dug-in Australian soldier carries out a kit inspection during a lull in the fighting for Tel-el-Eisa, 23 July 1942. The breech mechanism of his .303 Lee Enfield rifle is covered with sacking to prevent sand from entering the working parts. (E.14751)

blown to pieces. The infantry became separated from their tanks and when they arrived at their objectives there was no infantry support. This set the German back on their heels pretty solidly.

In the front line, Corporal Victor Knight found his Vickers machine-gun section (from 2/2nd Machine-Gun Battalion) involved in some of the heaviest fighting of the day. For 'utter disregard for [his] own safety' he was awarded the Distinguished Conduct Medal. He describes his part in repelling the German attack on 12 July:

They put in another attack with tanks, after blasting us with shells and bombs and Stukas which really bashed up our side of the hill. I brought the lads up and started to fire at them. Then one of my boys, Jimmy Nimmo – who'd been over the hill to pick up ammunition – said, 'Hey Vic, they're coming in from the other side.' So I scrambled up the hill and saw tanks and infantry coming in at the rear. I grabbed the blokes and took the guns over the other side – there was no cover – and began firing at the advancing Germans for about three hours. We had to urinate on the barrels to keep them cool enough to keep firing. We had oil available and we simply poured it from a four-gallon drum into the working parts, keeping the guns firing all the time.

By about 7 o'clock that night the Jerries were so close – within four or five hundred yards – that I turned the guns over to gun control, using what is known as a swing traverse so that they were firing under their own control. There was

nothing much for me to do except to move them backwards and forwards if the enemy artillery got onto them, or to give them new targets. So I grabbed myself a rifle and prepared to go in with the bayonet if the Germans got too close. Eventually their attack faded, leaving 600 dead on the slopes of Tel el Eisa.

The inability of the Germans to dislodge the Eighth Army marked the high-water mark of the Axis tide. The initiative passed over to Auchinleck, although any hopes the British had of throwing the Axis back were thwarted in turn by excellent German defensive tactics. On 22 July the battle stuttered to a close, both sides digging in and erecting defences across the desert choke point, running from Alamein down to the Qattara depression in the south.

Rommel knew that he must make one last effort to destroy the British before the pendulum of material forces swung irrevocably against him. The British, for their part, knew they had to hang on until reinforcements reached the battle front.

A British 4.5-inch gun fires at concentrations of Axis tanks and motor transport south of Alamein, 22/23 July 1942. The 4.5-inch gun had a good range in excess of 20,000 yards but its relatively light shell (55lb) compared poorly with the 5.5-inch gun (100lb) which was coming into service during this period. (E.14775)

115

Boxes and Jock Columns

The Bir Hakeim box shortly after its capture by Axis forces. As in other boxes the fortifications were basic: slit trenches connected to a few key strong points, surrounded by minefields. (MH.5872)

Despite their lack of desert experience the Germans learned quickly and their thorough appreciation of the dynamics of armoured warfare gave them a great advantage over their less adept British opponents. The panzers raced across the desert with a speed and flexibility that often proved too much for the British infantry; they would be caught in the open by German armour with predictably disastrous results.

A typically British response to the problem was the development of the infantry box, intended to provide the foot soldier with protection from the panzers. Boxes varied in size but the most usual was one what could hold an infantry brigade of three battalions along with artillery and engineers. The perimeter would consist of slit trenches to hold the infantry with some more elaborately constructed gun pits for the artillery. Around the perimeter would be a ring of barbed wire and then an extensive minefield.

That the box came to be a regular element of Eighth Army tactical thinking revealed a basic flaw in British military organization and doctrine. The British Army, like all other armies, utilized the divisional system. On paper this was a multi-arms formation able to operate independently on the battlefield; in reality this rarely happened. In fact, the British Army was based on the regimental system, which operated as a collection of separate units. Co-operation between these semi-tribal entities was not properly understood and in the extremes of combat regularly broke down.

The German concept of an armoured (panzer) division comprising an equal and mutually supporting combination of tanks, mechanized infantry, artillery, anti-tank guns and other supporting arms was unknown in practice to the British. In the Eighth Army a distinction between the separate arms was invariably maintained, especially between the infantry and armour.

A. H. G. Dobson was in the ill-fated 150 Brigade box; he highlights some of the weaknesses inherent in the boxes of the Gazala line:

We lived in those days in what were called defensive boxes which were supposed to be more or less self-contained, protected by the most enormous minefield of up to three or four miles across in front of us. It was thought to be virtually impregnable. In the event it didn't prove to be so.

The major problem was that the boxes were too far apart, so that when the great attack came at the end of May there just wasn't the co-ordination between adjacent boxes. The 69 Brigade box to our right must have been five miles away and on the other side the Free French box at Bir Hakeim must have been another five miles to our south. This lack of support meant one was really fighting an individual battle which was a disaster if Rommel decided to turn his full might on you – which is exactly what happened to our brigade.

Jock columns were another desert improvisation that developed into a tactical system. They were named after their inventor, Jock Campbell, a desert legend who earned a Victoria Cross for his inspired leadership during the battle of Sidi Rezegh and who was killed in a road accident shortly after assuming command of the 7th Armoured Division. The Jock column was a mixed force of vehicles, typically a few light tanks or armoured cars with guns and lorry-borne infantry. Harold Sell describes their function and composition during the period before Gazala:

Originator of the Jock column, Major-General Jock Campbell VC. (E.8262)

The job of a Jock column would be either to patrol an area and be sufficiently strong to take on any enemy reconnaissance unit, or go out on a specific mission such as beat up an enemy air strip or get some prisoners. Generally, the idea was to dominate the whole of No Man's Land between you and the Boche. They consisted of a company of infantry, a portee anti-tank attachment [two-pounder anti-tank guns mounted on the back of a lorry], some 25-pounders and carriers with 3-inch mortars. We might have South African Marmon Herrington armoured cars or light tanks called Honeys [M3 Stuarts] for back up.

An instance of a Jock column acting in an aggressive rather than reconnaissance role is provided in an account by Bob Braithwate, an RASC driver operating with a New Zealand unit:

A Jock column under air attack in the No Man's Land between British and Axis positions along the Gazala line, 30 March 1942. Wide dispersal of vehicles normally ensured that casualties were slight. (E.9947)

We were with the New Zealand Division and my truck had a mortar on board, a load of mortar bombs and a crew of five. We were detailed to go south into the desert for three days, then round and back up behind Jerry lines. The idea was to cut the supply route on the coast road at Bardia, where submarines and small ships were bringing arms, ammo and petrol for Rommel's panzers, now re-grouping around Tobruk.

We got there OK after a few skirmishes, either chasing Jerry patrols out of sight, or vice versa. The road was down on the three-mile wide coastal strip. We picked the escarpment ridge which ran alongside for five or six miles, just outside Bardia. The infantry dug in one the face of the cliff, about 100 feet high, well hidden.

We couldn't dig in – it was solid rock. We pick-axed a foot down and then built up a foot of rocks around our trench. The Kiwis had a line of about thirty Riflemen, with two Bren guns and two Vickers belt-fed machine-guns spaced out.

Nothing was seen for a couple of days. Then one morning we heard motor cycles coming from Bardia. It was a small convoy of three trucks with two BMW bikes at the front and rear. The Sergeant said quietly, 'Let them come right level with us. Don't shoot till I tell you, then the Vickers first, then Brens, then when you see them run, everybody blast them.'

Along they came in the bright sun, singing and shouting to each other, completely unaware of us. We were all on pins as usual – rifles cocked, just peeping over the rocks. It seemed as if they were going right past, then came the order 'Fire!' and Krrrrp went the Vickers at both ends. The front despatch rider's head left his body and dropped on the road behind: the body went on with the bike for a few yards, then careered into the other bike, the driver of which did not move – he was dead when he hit the ground.

The trucks slewed round. The first stopped immediately to avoid the bikes, the second pulled right on to the desert, accelerating in a cloud of dust.

A soldier from the 3rd South African Armoured Car Reconnaissance Battalion takes a bearing with a magnetic compass. Armoured cars – such as this South-African-assembled Marmon Herrington – were an integral part of Jock columns, intended to provide mobile fire-support. (E.10601)

'Twenty-fives on open sights!' went the shout to the four 25-pounders just behind us over the ridge. They wheeled 'em up, then 'Whoosh, whoosh, whoosh, whoosh!', all the trucks were stopped. The poor schickelgrubers scattered and ran. One went only three yards and crawled to a patch of scrub. He was almost invisible.

'Now, you rifle blokes – put your money where your mouths are. You're always saying how good you are. Get him!' The machine-guns had picked off the others who lay scattered, almost invisible in their light khaki desert clothes. 'Crack crack' went the rifles, but in three or four minutes there was no move or sign of a hit. It was approximately a $\frac{3}{4}$-mile shot to the road and in bright sun – very glary – so there was some excuse. But one shot got home and the poor beggar jumped up, limping, shouting, waving, running. 'Poor bastard,' said one Vickers man – and 'Crrack' he tumbled like a rag doll. Then all went quiet, hardly a sound or word, the dust settling, the flies buzzing, the heat building up.

The Corporal then said, 'Leave 'em. There'll be more soon now, once the word gets through.' Sure enough, that afternoon at dusk, out crept a column of one motor bike and sidecar, three old Eyetie tanks, and two trucks full of infantry. The boys blasted hell out of them, and what was left scarpered.

Although Jock columns were popular with junior officers because they gave them a chance to get away from the confines of regimental duties and to exercise independent command, they dissipated the strength of the Eighth Army – in direct contrast to the German principle of concentrating the armour and artillery within the panzer division. When out in No Man's Land the Jock column was vulnerable to ambush by superior German forces sent out to deal with these British nuisances. Sell relates one such incident:

We had a disaster with what we called Rosscol, commanded by Major Ross McLaren. The first thing we knew about it was a message from two or three men who had infiltrated the wire [of the 151 Brigade box] stating that the column had been overwhelmed four or five miles out in the desert. Immediately a relief column was sent out and discovered that Rosscol had been ambushed by German Mark IV tanks. They'd shot the whole lot up and, apart from a few survivors who'd made it back, they'd either killed or taken everyone prisoner, including Ross McLaren. That, of course, was a flap in the land of flaps.

During the same period before Rommel resumed his offensive on 26 May 1942, Bob Sykes was assigned to a Jock column:

We formed ourselves into a mobile self-supporting unit, with tanks, support vehicles, 25-pounder guns, Bofors [AA guns], machine-gun groups, anti-tank guns and infantry from the KRRC [King's Royal Rifle Corps]. We were to strike at the enemy flanks or even behind their lines, and take on enemy supply and support units. We would have the support of the Desert Air Force. This was to be our next role; it sounded all right but we were to be up against stronger enemy units with efficient equipment and armour. Once again it would be a cat and mouse game out in No Man's Land, with us completely cut off.

W. I. Watson who, like Sell, was an officer in the Durham Light Infantry, had considerable experience of the Jock column. On balance he was not impressed: 'I suppose they kept the chaps occupied when we were in a defensive position but I won't say they did a lot of good, other than keep the Germans on their toes.'

Prisoners of War

The desert campaigns were a war of movement and it was inevitable that there would be large numbers of men who, cut off from the main army, were captured and taken prisoner. Although a humiliating and often wretched experience, surrenders between the Axis and British forces were very rarely refused and the prisoners' lives were respected. On the British side the vast majority of prisoners were Italians, partly because their slow-moving infantry divisions were very vulnerable to capture and also because many Italians had little interest in 'Mussolini's quarrel' and were prepared to get out of the war via the POW cage.

During the first British offensive in 1940–41 over 130,000 Italian troops went into the bag. For British soldiers following in the wake of the advance, long columns of Italians making their way to the rear was a common sight of the campaign. Once overrun the Italians seemed only

A distinctive feature of the Desert War: long columns of Italian prisoners being led away to the rear. These men were captured in the opening phase of Wavell's Offensive, this photograph taken on 16 December 1940. (E.1376)

An Italian POW band in full swing in a camp in Egypt, 28 June 1941. (E.3893)

too keen to throw in the towel, especially since they knew of the good treatment they would be afforded by their captors. Lieutenant-Commander J. B. Lamb observed the progress of one such column:

Throughout the day more prisoners were coming in whilst others were being evacuated to the rear in captured motor transport. There was no cage for the 10,000 or so miserable Italians massed together, making a blue-grey smear on the desert face – crouching to get what little protection they could. Only a small guard was required because they had no inducement to escape.

A short while later, following the capture of Tobruk, Lamb encountered Italian prisoners of somewhat higher rank:

On the following forenoon the Italian admiral commanding at Tobruk and his chief of staff arrived to stay with us until they could be sent back to Cairo. The Italian officers were more than a little dazed by the turn of events, but were determined to put as good a face on it as possible. Neither bore any animosity and both were almost pathetically grateful for our small courtesies such as the loan of razors, a brush for their clothes, or the offer of a glass of wine.

Axis prisoners from the other ranks were used by the British authorities in Egypt as manual labour. Assigned to supervise gangs of prisoners, R. H. Kitson had a chance to compare the Italians with the few Germans who came his way:

I used Italian prisoners and they worked quite well, especially if you happened to get one who spoke a bit of English. We used them mainly on digging holes for telegraph poles or digging trenches for our cables. They were delighted if

German prisoners stand in line following their capture by Australian troops at the battle of Alamein, October 1942. (E.18494)

you went back to Alexandria to collect stores, because when they came with us we fed them with our rations which were better than they received in the prison camps. On one occasion I used German prisoners – but never again. You couldn't trust them and they were very arrogant. They wouldn't work, and if a man won't work then you can't make him.

For most men in the Eighth Army the interest in prisoners of war was limited to a concern over whether they themselves would end up in captivity. A. H. G. Dobson had been captured by a German unit following the destruction of the 150 Brigade box during the battle of Gazala:

They gave us water and that was a great relief. We were taken to a divisional headquarters (the 90th Light Division, I think) where they were very correct – no one can say anything else – although we had a fearful row about feeding our men, because by this time there were disarmed British soldiers lying about in every direction. They must have been an infernal nuisance to the Germans, made worse when officers like myself started demanding food for them. I thought, on the whole, the Germans behaved with considerable restraint and great propriety.

Bertram Martin was one of the 33,000 British and Dominion troops who marched into captivity from the Tobruk débâcle:

I was still with my regimental colleagues when I actually saw General Klopper [Major-General H. B. Klopper, GOC in Tobruk] go out with a white flag on his small truck and come back with a German staff car and then disappear in a dugout. When they came out one of the Germans fired a Very light into the sky which proved to be the signal for the German forces to move in. And we knew then that we were prisoners of war.

My impression of the Germans on the first day was that they were very generous as far as they could be. I received water from them – it was very scarce at the time – and a cigarette. I was quite impressed at the time with the German front-line soldier, as I think all my comrades were. We found out later that in the German Army, as with other armies, the front-line chap was OK but it was those who came afterwards who were less than desirable.

A few days after our capture a German got up on a soap box and told us that we were to be handed over to the Italians. He said: 'We don't like the Italians any more than you do but unfortunately these are our orders and we have to do this.'

The Italians lost no opportunity in humiliating us; they were cruel in that sense. Generally speaking, we didn't look upon the Italian as a very good soldier, and this was a reason for our dislike of them. Later on we found that any clothing they gave us would be already covered in lice so it was difficult keeping ourselves clean. And that didn't add to our opinion of them either.

I was reasonably fit before I got captured. I had had a little bout of dysentery when I first got to Egypt – that was only to be expected – but I suffered a really bad bout after I was captured because of the bad food given to us. It was about six weeks before I fully recovered to make my way to Italy.

We were taken to the ship and battened down in our hundreds. There were no toilet facilities at all. It was absolutely atrocious; three or four days of sheer hell. In the boat it was completely dark and it was so crowded that if you moved your leg you found someone else's leg. It was the done thing to urinate in your boot, there was nowhere else to go. When we eventually got off the boat in Naples we only just had enough strength to walk.

Martin's experience of the 'correct' behaviour of his German captors comparing favourably with the poor treatment meted out by the Italians is borne out in numerous testimonies from British prisoners in North Africa. For the most part it would seem that the Italian attitude towards prisoners was only rarely avowedly malicious, rather that the monumental inefficiency of the Italian military system led to indifference which in turn caused hardship for the men in the cages. Of course, this was little consolation for the prisoners themselves, and was a cause of lasting bitterness to some.

Harold Fitzjohn had fallen back from the Gazala battlefield to Tobruk where he was captured by a German reconnaissance unit. The German officer apologized for having to hand them over to the Italians. Once in Italian custody Fitzjohn and his fellow prisoners began to suffer ill-treatment. They were taken to a wire encampment in Derna:

A comic-opera Italian officer came along, all dolled up with his fancy boots gleaming away, and he started to take photographs of us all. The reaction was quick – immediately he put his camera up to take the picture everybody gave the V for Victory sign. After a few attempts he lost his temper and pulled out a revolver and threatened us with it. Once again all our fingers went up. So he just let off three shots into the midst of us. One lad was wounded in the arm, though the other two shots didn't hit anybody. I don't know whether he'd

Severely dehydrated Italian soldiers photographed on their capture by New Zealanders during the first battle of Alamein, 14 July 1942. Left stranded during the fighting for Ruweisat ridge the Italians' water had run out so, ironically, their capture brought them deliverance. (E.14622)

intended to fire over our heads and it was an accident or whether he'd deliberately aimed at us, but that was my introduction to the Italian Army.

While at Derna, Fitzjohn observed the poor relations which existed between the Germans and their erstwhile Italian allies: 'On one occasion an Italian soldier was trying to sell a bottle of water over the wire to one of our prisoners for an Egyptian pound. A German came along and took the bottle off the Italian and just threw it over the wire to the English prisoners.' From Derna Fitzjohn was taken back to Benghazi where conditions were even worse: dirty water, inadequate food and no proper medical facilities for the many diseases caused by such conditions. His final comment on the Italians: 'I've detested them ever since.'

Phil Loffman, an Australian infantryman of the 2/28th Battalion, was captured during the closing stages of the first battle of Alamein on 27 July 1942. The 2/28th had been fighting to gain control of the Miteiriya/Ruin Ridge when it was overrun by elements of the German 90th Light Division:

As soon as first light was over the sand hills, in they came. They were like cockroaches coming across the hills. It didn't last very long – you can't do much against tanks with just small arms ammunition. The fellow that actually got me was in a half-track, and in perfect English he said, 'Get out you English swine before I blast you out'. At this stage of the game I was wearing a Luger I'd

Two British prisoners are removed from the front in a German Kubel car. Most captures were made by the Germans who on the basis of an Axis agreement handed them over to Italian jurisdiction. The treatment of British prisoners by the Germans was generally very good, and was reciprocated by the British – a factor which helped make the campaigns in the desert among the more chivalrous of the Second World War. (HU.5605)

captured on a previous show, and someone had told me that if they caught you with a Luger they shot you with it. I was at the back of the trench trying to dig a hole and bury the Luger, but the bloke could see that I was doing something and I thought, 'Well, my God, I'll just have to leave it there.' It was either the Luger or the big Spandau [machine-gun] on the front of the half-track. I got out and put my hands up, and he came out with the old expression: 'For you the war is over.' What a lot of crap. For me the war had only started; this was just the beginning.

They rounded us up and took us to transit camps and cages where we stayed for about a month. The last one I was in was a place called the Palms in Benghazi. It was no oasis; it was a dry sandy hole with no buildings in it. The sun was hot in the daytime and the nights were cold. The Italian guards were a bomb happy lot. They used to get drunk on Chianti at night, and for fun they'd shoot into the compound. One of our blokes was caught trying to get out. They had him wired up to the gate as a crucifix figure, like Christ. I believe the Germans came round and made them take him down. But it wasn't long before we made the trip from Benghazi across to Italy.

Major L. Melzer, in command of a South African field ambulance during the Crusader battle of November 1941, had similar experiences when he and his command were overrun by Axis forces. He noted that on 30 November:

The whole hospital was taken over by the Italians and from that moment we were subjected to systematic thieving and looting. A parade of every able-bodied man was immediately called for and while they were at this parade, their belongings were searched and their sleeping quarters ransacked. Everything of

value was taken by the Italians and when I protested I was told the same thing was done to them by the Australians.

British prisoners in a transit camp somewhere in North Africa await shipment to permanent POW camps in Italy. (MH.5563)

Melzer's unit was liberated by the arrival of British forces a few days later. When Harold Harper of the South Notts Hussars had been captured at a Field Dressing Station during the battle of Gazala (*see page* 98) he believed that he too might be freed as a result of a reversal in Axis fortunes. Failing that he decided that he would attempt to escape as his wounds were not severe.

While he waited on events, Harper did his best to glean as much intelligence on the enemy as possible, noting down the movement and numbers of tank units as they swept past his dressing station: 'I kept my eye open for what was going on, for example, the tanks used purple smoke – every time their planes came over they puffed out some purple smoke to indicate who they were.'

When all reasonable hope of rescue had faded, Harper and a Welsh sergeant decided to escape. They slipped past their captors at the dressing station and began to march across the desert in the direction of the British lines. The sergeant was killed walking on a mine – 'there was hardly anything left of him' – but Harper was unhurt and carried on.

Water soon became a problem. A few drops were extracted from the radiators of abandoned vehicles but this was insufficient: 'I was desperate for water and eventually I had to drink my own urine. I started by swilling my mouth out and hoping for the best.' Fortunately, soon afterwards Harper was picked up by a British patrol and after recuperating from his ordeal he was able to pass on his information to British intelligence.

Harold Harper was something of an exception. Most prisoners had no chance to escape or were too exhausted by the conditions leading up to capture to consider the possibility of getting away. The vast majority were shipped over to Italian POW camps where they stayed until the Italian surrender in July 1943. As their guards simply walked away on receiving news of the armistice, some British prisoners managed to escape into the countryside and make their way to Allied lines or neutral Switzerland. Others were less fortunate and were promptly rounded up by the Germans and transported north to the Reich where they were held until the end of the war.

The Commonwealth Contribution

As in 1914, the Commonwealth was not slow to support Britain on the outbreak of war in 1939. Although the Commonwealth nations had made tentative steps towards greater independence of action in the interwar years, the political, economic, social and emotional ties with Britain were still strong. The Commonwealth commitment to the war in the Western Desert was considerable: 6th and 9th Australian Infantry Divisions, the New Zealand Division, 1st and 2nd South African Divisions, as well as naval and aviation units.

The military relationship between the Commonwealth and Britain was often stormy, however, reflecting differing military priorities. One constant source of friction between the Commonwealth generals and the British Commanders-in-Chief lay in the deployment of their forces. The British wanted to usc Commonwealth formations as they did their

A section of South African troops returns to base after a patrol through deep sand dunes, 21 July 1941. (E.4350)

Major-General Douglas Wimberley (second left) discusses plans with his staff during the Alamein follow-up. Wimberley's GSO-1, Roy Urquhart, looks on (left). Wimberley held the Commonwealth divisions in high esteem, especially the Australians with whom his Scottish troops had trained in preparation for the Alamein battle. (E.19362)

own, sending them where they thought best and splitting them up if necessary. The Commonwealth commanders were steadfastly – and understandably – opposed to any division of their forces, and always held the trump card of being able to refer back to their home governments if they were unhappy about accepting a British order. The High Command was clearly made aware that the Commonwealth divisions were not British formations to do with as they pleased.

Major-General Douglas Wimberley had recently arrived in Egypt with his 51st (Highland) Division in July 1942 when he encountered a low point in British-Commonwealth relations:

While in the desert I attended, as a spectator, a corps conference held by Ramsden [Major-General W. H. C. Ramsden, briefly GOC XXX Corps] and it was very clear that there was not inconsiderable friction and querying of orders by Dominion divisional commanders, doing what Monty would call 'belly-aching'. Each one said that before they could comply with certain orders they would have to contact their own Dominion governments. I remember when I left the conference saying to Roy Urquhart, my GSO1 [General Staff Officer–1 – subsequently to command the 1st Airborne Division at Arnhem] that the sooner I got in touch with the Secretary of State for Scotland the better.

While the Commonwealth regarded it as imperative that they maintain their forces in being, from a British perspective – with the Germans only sixty miles from Suez – it could look like bloody-minded intransigence.

The problem was never, nor could be, satisfactorily resolved; it was inevitably a question of compromise. Writing after the war to Gavin Long, the Australian Official Historian, the distinguished New Zealand soldier Major-General Sir Howard Kippenberger revealed his sympathy for the British predicament:

Wavell and Auchinleck must often have wished that they had only troops who would do what they were told without arguing. Freyberg [then Major-General B. C. Freyberg VC, GOC New Zealand Division] didn't like the way Crusader was run, didn't like the Ras el Ali project of the plan for Turkey or the brigade group theory, thought it might be better for someone else to be shut up in [Mersa] Matruh, had previously reacted violently to the suggestion that we should relieve 9th Australian Division in Tobruk, in fact always had some objection or counter-suggestion. I don't see that your people were always more easier handling. We may have been right, but I think only British commanders would have put up with us and hope we were worth the trouble. Undoubtedly we were.

The Australians had a high regard for the fighting qualities of their own troops which for the most part was amply justified. Major Charles Finlay of the 26th Brigade, 9th Australian Infantry Division, had no doubts as to the essential qualities of the 'Digger':

Discipline has different connotations for different people. The Australian 'Digger' had the discipline which allowed him to think and not do things automatically. The battle discipline of the AIF [Australian Imperial Force] in the Middle East was fantastic. That's why the Australians at El Alamein and Tel el Eisa always got their objectives, whereas some of the British and South African troops didn't because their battle discipline was inadequate. What I mean by that is the Australian private soldier understood what was required of him and what his duty was, and didn't have to wait for the section or platoon commander to issue him with orders.

Peter Jeffrey of No. 3 Squadron RAAF held a similar view of the respective merits of the Australian and British fighting man:

I don't think that the 'Pommy' was a softie in any shape or form; I think he was a very brave man and I think he put up with all sorts of conditions. I think the main difference was he just didn't have the initiative; he waited to be told, instead of getting on himself.

The quality of Australian battle discipline impressed most British observers. Jack Daniel wrote: 'There are two sorts of discipline, the Guards style, which we later admired so much which was British discipline, and the Australian sort, which was a non-discipline but was just as effective.' Frank Knowles of the South Notts Hussars considered the Australians to be 'great comrades, generous to a fault. For them, the normal understanding of Army discipline didn't exist, but there was an effective control system.' Harold Harper, also from the South Notts Hussars, recorded a dissenting view, however:

Their approach to military life differed – far less discipline than we had. A lot of their casualties were quite unnecessary in my opinion, because of their indiscip-

Australian reinforcements (in bush hats) meet up with British soldiers during the first battle of Alamein, 13 July 1942. Although the photograph was staged, it does reflect the generally good relations that existed between Commonwealth and British troops. (E.14303)

line. They would go into a situation fearlessly – let's be fair, they were fearless soldiers – but without adopting the correct tactical methods of approach shown by the British infantryman.

Australians had their views on the British. Jack Griffiths, from New South Wales, volunteered on 5 June to 'stop Hitler and help the mother country'. Posted to the 2/1 Pioneer Battalion he worked alongside the British during the siege of Tobruk. His comment: 'There was no difference between us. We were all under the same conditions with one purpose. In a lot of cases you couldn't tell who was who, there was no regimental dress. We got on very well together.'

Major-General Leslie Morshead, GOC of the 9th Australian Infantry Division, wrote this fulsome letter of appreciation to the Royal Horse Artillery which had fought alongside the Australians at Tobruk:

An example of Australian gallows humour on a roadside leading up to the front on the north of the Alamein line, August 1942.

Throughout our service in Tobruk, we have admired your high standard of technical efficiency; the ever-vigilant and alert observation posts; the ready response from the guns and the ease of co-operation with you. We realize what it means for guns to be continually in action day and night in all conditions of weather and without respite. You have given of your best. It has been magnificent and worthy of the traditions of your famous regiment.

Morshead had a less complimentary view of British armour and by July 1942 had growing doubts about British leadership in general. Douglas Wimberley's division had been posted alongside the Australians to be instructed by them in the techniques of desert warfare. When they met, Morshead made his feelings known to Wimberley, who entered these comments into his diary:

The next night I spent with Leslie Morshead. He was very kind and gave me a

Australian gunners crouch down beside a 6-pounder anti-tank gun, its barrel at full recoil. Introduced during the summer of 1942 the 6-pounder was the first effective anti-tank gun to be used by the British and Commonwealth forces in North Africa; its ability to penetrate up to 2.7 inches of armour at 1000 yards rendered all Axis tanks vulnerable. (E.14386)

lot of sound advice. It was clear from talking to him that the Australians did not have a very high regard for the British armour, which they thought had let them down. He told me that the staff were mad on breaking divisions up into 'Jock' columns and that if I allowed them to break my division up I would never be able to collect it together again. He very firmly resisted any attempt to 'muck about' with his Australians. I took a great liking to Morshead right away, and he gave me a feeling of higher morale than I had yet seen in the Eighth Army.

The Australians readily admitted that spit and polish soldiering meant little to them. For the British soldier their informality could be variously irritating, amusing or very refreshing. During the siege of Tobruk, L. E. Tutt was sent out to an Australian-manned observation post, along with an officer of small stature, nicknamed Croucher:

It was the first time that I had observed the easy relationship that existed between the Australian men and their officers. We arrived without difficulty, jumping down into the circular weapon pit from which they kept the enemy under close observation. One of the chaps on duty said, 'Good on you, mates,' and then turning to Croucher, 'Give us your gear, Shortarse.' I expected all hell to break loose but our officer, who had been in the OP before, just grinned.

Once I heard the following conversation between the officer in charge of the post and the private who combined fighting with being his batman. The private: 'Look here, Norm, you take your bloody turn emptying the dixie or you'll get no bloody char.' The officer's reply: 'Stuff you, Snow. It ain't my bloody turn again.'

The relaxed Australian approach extended right up the scale, as Major-General Wimberley discovered:

I went round a sector of the line held by Australian soldiers. They were all half naked and as brown as berries. They took a bit of getting used to. I was dressed as a general yet they treated me in a most 'matey' way, but despite this it was easy to see that there was nothing wrong with their battle discipline. Their weapons were clean and ready to use and their sentries were alert.

The Australians, like all troops, had their weaknesses. During the siege of Tobruk the strain took its toll on the defenders' morale. Sergeant J. R. Oates of the Australian Military History Section based in Tobruk wrote this summary prepared from monthly reports by Major D. J. Benjamin, the Legal Staff Officer of the 9th Division:

The lapses in discipline at Tobruk were caused mainly by the strains of war. Besides constant air raids and shelling, the troops were affected by a mental attitude of frustration not unlike claustrophobia.

There were many cases of desertion and a smaller number of self-inflicted wounds. Some cases of desertion could be attributed to a 'bomb-happy' state in much the same manner as shell-shock in the 1914–18 war, and others were possibly due to plain fear. Many of the SIW [self-inflicted wound] cases were not wilfully brought about. They were clearly caused by negligence. Such negligence could result from over-anxiety. It was found that men did not follow out the elementary safety precautions when cleaning rifles.

It may be noted that stealing and desertion cases occurred also among the British personnel at Tobruk. They had fewer SIW cases, but they were mostly serving in rear areas, whereas most of the Australians were in the front line. There was plenty of stealing in Tobruk because opportunities were almost unlimited.

Away from the front line the Digger's vigorous approach to life caused problems for the authorities. Better paid than their British equivalents, Australian troops sometimes engaged in orgies of drunkenness. On one occasion an intoxicated Australian soldier accosted British general officers, an incident that led to a heated exchange between the British Army commander and the Australian divisional general. L. E. Tutt draws this, perhaps exaggerated, picture of the Aussie enjoying rest and recreation:

They were the bane of provost marshals when they were on leave. They burnt trams without necessarily bothering to see if all the passengers were out of them first. They tended to react to overcharging by throwing the bar proprietors through their plate glass windows.

A group of us were drinking with them in an establishment in Cairo called Madam Bardia's. Their provost marshal came in with a team of military policemen to remove some of the more obviously drunk. To a man the whole place erupted in protest against authority: bottles, glasses, chairs, tables, even waiters were hurled through the air at the punitive party, which was forced to retire. They returned with about fifty Australian MPs who went into action against their own men, clubbing them into insensibility and carting away their bodies in jeeps.

A scene in a New Zealand forward headquarters, taken by Cecil Beaton (*see also* photograph on page 49). Disciplined informality characterized the New Zealand approach to warfare. (CBM.1424)

Whatever their failings in the recreational field, the Australians had an excellent overall fighting record in North Africa, beginning with the assault on Bardia, through the siege of Tobruk to the battles of Alamein. An interesting perspective is provided by an observer from the 'other side of the hill'. Major Ballerstedt commanded an infantry battalion besieging Tobruk in 1941 and he wrote this report on the troops facing him: 'The Australians are extraordinarily tough fighters. The German is more active in the attack but the enemy stakes his life in the defence and fights to the last with extreme cunning. Our men, usually easygoing and unsuspecting, easily fall into his traps.'

The New Zealand Division had a similarly high reputation among British forces in North Africa. Although the division suffered a serious reverse at First Alamein – in part due to lack of support from British armour – its performance during Operation Crusader was exceptional. Despite suffering heavy casualties – 4620 men, higher than any other division – and for much of the time operating almost alone on the coastal sector, the New Zealand Division fought with the greatest determina-

tion. J. E. Brooks, a British gunner attached to the New Zealand Division, made this comment when he heard that his unit was to be transferred to a British division: 'We wished we were going with the New Zealanders. They are a grand lot of chaps and we were always glad to be with them.'

As in the Australian formations, the officer–man relationship was a generally relaxed one, as the following two quotations suggest:

Most New Zealanders had a great respect for their officers and regarded them as equals. Senior rather than superior. I believe this was fully understood and reciprocated by most New Zealand officers and contributed a great deal to the efficiency of the division.

Discipline in line was good because you didn't have a great difference between men and officers. Where officers were killed you had men who could take over. Regardless of rank, most men are equal when it comes to war combat. This would account for the mutual respect of officers to their men – hence Christian name terms.

2nd Lieutenant Charles Upham of the New Zealand Division is congratulated by his men on the news of his award of a Victoria Cross for an action in Crete. Extraordinarily, Upham was to win a second VC in the Western Desert – the only time a bar to the VC has been gained which was not posthumous. (E.6067)

137

A fine portrait of a soldier in a
Sikh regiment, taken in
Egypt, 1 May 1941. Indian
Army troops fought with
distinction in all the battles of
the Desert War. (E.2717E)

Such familiarity would have been unheard of in British regiments,
arguably to their disadvantage.

South African forces had played an important part in the conquest of
Italian East Africa in 1941. Thereafter two divisions served in North
Africa. Under strength and lacking in experienced leadership they fared
less well than the Australians and New Zealanders. Particularly unfortunate was the surrender at Tobruk, which saw the 2nd Division
marched off into captivity. In many respects the South Africans were
victims of the confusion following on from the defeat at Gazala but there
can be little doubt that uninspired South African generalship contributed to the disaster.

Comparisons with the earlier siege – and the fine Australian perform-ance there – were inevitably made, to the South Africans' disadvantage. F. M. V. Tregear, a British officer present at the siege, made this scathing comment: 'The tragic history of Tobruk was a blunder of the greatest magnitude from first to last. Muddled thinking was combined with the crass incompetence of a buffoon. Altogether a humiliating disgrace, not to mention betrayal of the Eighth Army."

Despite this setback the South Africans fought well in both the Alamein battles, while their armoured car regiments earned a fine reputation for boldness and enterprise during operations on the south-ern, desert flank. Intelligence officer R. H. Dahl was posted to a South African armoured car squadron in the period after First Alamein. He made this comment: 'The South African soldiers had been hardened by long desert experience and developed an aggressive fighting philosophy. They were always loath to withdraw from any engagement.'

Soldiers from the Commonwealth – particularly Australia – con-sidered themselves to be an elite within the Eighth Army. Assessing the performance and character of a nation's armed forces is always fraught with danger, relying so heavily on the subjective element. Some of the old myths of the Commonwealth soldier, which exaggerated his military prowess vis-à-vis the downtrodden British soldier and made out the British High Command to be a gang of cynical butchers, have recently been demolished.[1] A younger generation of Commonwealth historians has begun the task of stripping away the varnish of accumulated myth to present a more honest picture of their nations' armed forces.

From the viewpoint of most British soldiers serving in the field, the Australians, New Zealanders and South Africans made a magnificent contribution to the defeat of the Axis armies in North Africa, an effort remembered with admiration and wry affection.

Lastly, some mention should be made of the Indian troops who fought in North Africa. The Indian Army could hardly be considered as a colonial force but as part of the British Empire its status was very different from that of the Commonwealth formations. The composition of the Indian Army reflected this anomalous position: each brigade was composed of one British battalion alongside two Indian battalions while artillery and other services came from both British and Indian sources. Senior officers were still British although at regimental level there was a mix of Indian and British. The 4th Indian Division played an important part in the opening of Wavell's Offensive in December 1940; the 5th and 10th divisions in the summer battles of 1942; and the 4th Division again from the battle of Alamein on to Tunisia.

[1] See, for example, John McLeod's *Myth and Reality: The New Zealand Soldier in World War II* (Heinemann Reed, Auckland, 1986)

PART FIVE

WAR IN THE AIR

'After the first attack four of our chaps dived down to the ships while five of us stayed up top to keep the 109s busy. Our pilots were just in time as they caught the twenty Stukas sneaking in on the ships. They piled in, broke up the attack and shot down five bombers'.

COMMANDING OFFICER, *SAAF Fighter Squadron*

The War in the Air

For both sides the air war in North Africa remained a theatre of secondary importance, strategic concerns elsewhere demanding the lion's share of resources. The British and Commonwealth Desert Air Force came to regard itself as a Cinderella service. Not only were aircraft in short supply but the models they received were obsolete by the standards of other theatres. Fortunately for the British, while the German air contingent had better quality machines – in particular the Messerschmitt Bf-109 fighter which was far superior to the Hurricanes and Tomahawks of the RAF – their numbers were insufficient to tip the balance in their favour.

The prime function of the Desert Air Force was to support the ground forces and so its main roles were ground attack and air defence against Axis bombers and their fighter protection. In addition there were a few squadrons of medium bombers for longer range interdiction attacks against convoys, ports and other supply centres.

The quality of machinery apart, the Air Force suffered from the climatic conditions imposed by the desert. Gone were the tarmac runways and cushy billets of air operations in Britain, replaced instead by rough sand strips and canvas tents. Even though conditions were unpleasant for the men, it was the machines that were affected most. Group-Captain (later Air Chief Marshal Sir Frederick) Rosier was in command of a fighter wing in North Africa and he explained some of the problems encountered there:

It was the aeroplanes that suffered, above all from the sand. We eventually got these filters, called Volkes filters, to stop the ingestion of sand but they affected the performance of the aeroplane. Hurricanes fitted with Volkes filters were awful compared, for example, with the German Messerschmitt 109Es and 109Fs.

Shortages of supplies and difficult working conditions made the ground crews' job particularly difficult. Hard work and ingenuity solved most of these problems. Peter Jeffrey, a pilot and later commander of 3 Squadron Royal Australian Air Force (RAAF), commended his crewmen:

They were first-class technicians who got on with the job and didn't need to be instructed in detail. They showed a terrific amount of initiative. To quote an example: some of the Italian aircraft had a Bristol engine which was made under licence in Italy and it took our coves no time at all to find out they were exactly the same as the engines in the Gladiators, and so we had spare parts from crashed Italian aircraft.

R. H. 'Bobby' Gibbes commanded 3 Squadron RAAF (later in the war).

He too came to admire his airmen's ability to scrounge and acquire non-regulation items – the practice of 'cliftying':

Three Squadron was known as the 'clifty' squadron. We had double the amount of transport that we were entitled to. We had German trucks, Italian trucks and when there was going to be an inspection, we'd get a warning – we'd have friends in high places – that our transport was going to be looked at. And you'd see little dust trails going off in all directions out into the desert until the inspection was over, while the official vehicles would stay put.

The easy-going approach to discipline that was to become a trademark of the Australian forces sometimes extended to British squadrons as well. On arriving to take command of 252 Fighter Wing, Group-Captain G. V. Howard was not impressed by what he saw: 'Very shaken to see primitive manner in which the men live. The tents are very untidy and no attempt has been made to lift the flaps daily. I can see there is a lot of uphill work to be faced.' Howard's disapproval extended to what he considered his pilots' poor flight and tactical discipline, made worse by their reaction to his criticism over a particular incident: 'They endeavoured to argue when I told 'em they made a mistake attacking in succession instead of in concert. In effect, the discipline is damned bad!'

Despite the many privations experienced by the airmen out in 'the

A squadron of the South African Air Force cheers its 101st kill, the score chalked on the fuselage of a captured Italian CR-42 biplane, 9 June 1941. (E.3114)

An Australian pilot stands astride his Kittyhawk ground-attack aircraft. The Kittyhawk was the RAF description for the P-40D (and all later versions), and was distinguished from the Tomahawk by its larger chin radiator. (CM.3602)

Blue', many crews liked the rugged outdoor life that the desert provided – and its unique peace and quiet. Richard de Yarburgh-Bateson (later Lord Deramore) was a sergeant-observer on night bombers. Following in the wake of the Allied victory at Alamein, he gives this lyrical description of his forward airfield in a diary entry for 6 December 1942:

It is certainly cooler now. I sit on my bed wearing long khaki-drill trousers, battle-dress jacket and desert shoes. An Irvin jacket is spread over my knees. Outside the sand is the same ruddy yellow, but the sky is a paler blue than in mid-summer and partially screened by cirrus and stratus clouds. The mountains raise their rugged grey-brown flanks in the middle distance, while the monotony of the foreground is only relieved by the sandbagged bays and numerous aircraft, some of whose engines are roaring angrily, their propellors blowing clouds of sand dust behind them. Some are black with the sinister intent of the night bomber, their bellies bulging earthwards, pregnant with destruction. Others are the blue-grey of the coastal air force. These are sleeker

and lighter looking, and carry slender blue torpedoes slung negligently beneath the fuselage.

One important responsibility for the fighter units was to provide aerial support for the many British convoys making their way across the Mediterranean. The CO of a South African squadron flying Hurricanes provided this story of his adventures as a convoy escort:

I was leading the formation on patrol one evening, escorting a convoy some distance out to sea. We were nearing the end of our patrol and about to leave when a formation of twenty Messerschmitt fighters passed over about 2000 feet above us. The Germans' tactics were to send out fighters first to draw our fighters away from the ships in order that the more vulnerable dive bombers could lay their eggs in comparative safety.

Our aircraft had of course to protect the ships by staying over them. When the 109s passed overhead we got on our toes and turned towards them. They started to dive down in waves. It was at this stage that two of our chaps put up a marvellous show: their duty was to break up the main attack. The two of them pitched straight into the Germans without hesitation and scattered them satisfactorily. Unfortunately they both went missing that day. I picked a 109 and did a head-on attack on him. I gave him a good squirt. My half-section who was flying behind me – guarding my tail – saw him pull up, turn and then dive into the sea. Evidently the pilot had been hit.

Things now began to move pretty fast. After the first attack four of our chaps

A formation of British Hurricane II fighters flies through the clouds over the Western Desert. Although slow as a fighter the Hurricane was manoeuverable and could absorb a good degree of punishment. (CM.3638)

dived down to the ships while five of us stayed up top to keep the 109s busy. Our pilots were just in time as they caught the twenty Stukas sneaking in on the ships. They piled in, broke up the attack and shot down five bombers. This was confirmed later by reports from the ships who saw the whole show. Some of the bombs fell near the ships while others were jettisoned far away by Stuka pilots who discarded all ideas of attack and urged every ounce of speed from their unfortunate aircraft in order to get away.

The ships were still steaming away undamaged as we left. It was pretty dark by then – you feel very lonely at that time in the evening when you are some forty miles out to sea. You can hardly imagine how good the coast looks when it finally shows up.

The aggressive attitude displayed by the Desert Air Force fighter units was commented upon at the time. Rosier noted that 'even when we were suffering quite heavy casualties – and we did – we had an offensive spirit the whole time. In fact, the Germans couldn't take it.' The next account from an anonymous wing-commander exemplifies this approach to the full:

Today we were rewarded for the hours we've spent sitting around waiting for the Hun to take the plunge and pay us a visit. Pilots representing every country in the Empire got away to a good start and caught the Hun as he beat it for home. There were equal numbers of fighters on either side but for a change the Hun was tied down, having had to escort his Stukas.

Then began a dogfight such as I have rarely ever been lucky to know. It was shades of the last war; the greatest fun in the world. The Hun was forced to fight at our level – there were 109s, Tomahawks, Stukas and Kittyhawks going spare in all directions. It was a wonderful sight with plenty of action; aircraft crash landing on the coast, parachutes floating down and aircraft diving into the sea only added to the excitement.

After about twenty minutes of this dogfight we turned for home in twos or threes, having used up all our ammunition. And so it was back to base to shoot a line to those poor wretches whom we had left on the ground. At the close of play, the score was well in our favour. For many of the pilots it was their first real free-for-all and they came up to the highest expectations. All agreed it was a grand morning. The main thing, however, was that we now had pilots who had tasted blood, liked it and wanted more.

From the ground a dogfight seemed to be an even more confusing mêlée than it did in the air. During the retreat back to Alamein in July 1942, Dr Theodore Stephanides observed a spectacular aerial scrap between the Luftwaffe and the Desert Air Force:

About 6pm we heard some very heavy bombing about a mile south-east of us and saw about twenty German bombers, protected by fighters, circling above a convoy of vehicles strung out across the desert. I could see huge bursts of smoke and debris leaping up from the ground until they formed a long grey curtain that half hid the vehicles. At first it looked as if the Germans were having it all their own way, when I noticed another group of about twenty of our planes approaching. This was the first air battle I had seen in which both sides were in approximately equal numbers.

Then suddenly – so suddenly that I was taken completely by surprise – the

whole sky seemed to be full of planes wheeling round about one another with their cannon and machine-guns blazing. I had always thought that, in modern air fighting, both sides kept some sort of formation in a big battle. But there was nothing like that here. Planes were just circling and weaving in and out among each other, reminding me of a flock of seagulls when a bucket of swill has been emptied over a ship's side.

Within scarcely a minute of the beginning of the fight, four planes had crashed in flames. They fell blazing in a row, about a mile to the east of us, and four tall columns of black smoke gushed up into the sky. The rest of the fight swept right over our heads, and soon we were leaping for cover as stray bullets streaked unpleasantly close to us, kicking up the sand in every direction.

The rest of the mêlée had swept past, the Germans fleeing and the British pursuing, and before we could believe it possible the skies were empty again. The four columns of black smoke with a red glow at their base were the only signs that any fight had taken place. All fire, fury and pandemonium one minute, and silence and emptiness the next. A good example of the headlong pace of modern warfare – the First World War air battles had been leisurely encounters by comparison.

Fighter leaders on both sides tried to gain the tactical edge over their opponents. The Germans had always used the *Schwarm* of four planes divided into two pairs which was a far superior tactical unit to the awkward Vic-3 system of the British, involving three aircraft in a V formation. By the end of 1940 the Desert Air Force was dispensing with the Vic-3 for groups of pairs – a leader and his wingman. Bobby Gibbes:

We evolved what we called 'weaving pairs'. The Germans used to call us the 'Waltzing Matildas'. Each pair – we generally flew in sixes, in three pairs – would be weaving in flight, except the leader of the six. When we came to do a turn, the ones on the outside would dive under the leader and the ones on the inside would go on to the other side. It worked out beautifully – you'd maintain position without having to change your throttle setting, and that was pretty good.

Improvements in tactics would be negated if the quality of the individual pilots was poor. Frederick Rosier listed the qualities required for successful aerial combat:

The good fighter pilot must have pretty good eyesight. If you can see things before the others, you're at a great advantage. You must also have a good head, be able to assess how much time you've got and be able to look round the sky and take it all in. The average chap can only take in a certain amount at any one time. The good fighter pilot can take a lot in. Lastly, of course, is the ability to aim and shoot well.

For pilots forced down in the desert, getting back to their own lines was a major problem – especially if injured or wounded. For those that did manage to walk home an unofficial club was set up, complete with a winged boot badge. One such club member was a Free French pilot, Lieutenant Pompei, whose plane was shot up in a dogfight over enemy lines on 4 December 1941:

I tried to make for the coast with three Jerries on my tail, with a badly crippled plane. I reached the coast and was still at 2000 feet when the engine gave way. I crash-landed with my wheels up on a piece of flat rock. I managed to get out and began limping towards the east. After a few minutes some Arabs called to me. At first I didn't answer but as they were armed I had to stop. They gave me the fascist salute and asked 'Italiano?' I shook my head. 'Germani?' 'No.' 'Inglesi?' 'Yes.' At this they were delighted. They carried me to their tent a few hundred yards away, looked after me and got out of my leg some sixty shell splinters with the needle they use to sew their tents. It was very well done.

   I stayed with them for three weeks and there was never an attempt to give me away. They hated the Italians and never missed an opportunity to take a shot at one. Eventually they decided to send me back to British lines and a caravan of 104 camels was diverted to take me on my way. On the journey we passed within two hundred yards of a German patrol, clearly visible in the moonlight.

   Then my guides took me to a 2000-year old vault while a shepherd took a message to our lines. I learned later that the shepherd, who was an old man of seventy-four, travelled ninety miles in two days. At last he met a friendly armoured car which took him to a British intelligence officer, and a motorized patrol was sent to fetch me. My arrival came as quite a surprise to my comrades who had thought I was dead.

By early 1942 both sides were making full use of radar to track approaching enemy bomber formations. The enterprising Rosier was

Captain Kok of the South African Air Force displays his winged-boot badge, awarded to pilots who managed to regain their own lines after being shot down over enemy territory. (E.3301E)

able to employ radar and his radio-intercept unit to good effect on an occasion during March 1942 when his planes were grounded:

I was based at El Adem with the controllers of the fighter group. We had a radar forward at Gazala but the rains had come and our airfields were all mud, preventing us from operating at all. We heard from our local Y unit (which listened in to enemy radar and radio transmissions) that it appeared as though there was going to be a raid. The next thing we knew was that it would be Italian Stukas, escorted by German 109s.

Suddenly I had an idea. I rang up the radar station at Gazala and said, 'You will hear us giving certain orders on the radio. As soon as you hear any order from us you are to reply "Roger".' If they gave lengthy transmissions the German direction-finding units would know that their transmissions were coming from the radar station.

I then decided to send some imaginary fighters into the air. The Y section continued to give us information and it wasn't long before the radar station at Gazala also told us they'd picked up the raid coming in on their radar. I then 'scrambled' the imaginary fighters and gave them orders to climb. The next thing I heard from our Y unit was that German Y units had picked up my transmissions and had told the raid – the Stukas and 109s – that the British had sent up some fighters to intercept them.

The commander of the Desert Air Force, Air Vice-Marshal Sir Arthur Coningham (far left) confers with senior officers responsible for fighter activity over the Western Desert. Frederick Rosier is third from left, in chair. (CM.2923)

I continued to vector our fighters. When they were supposedly pretty close to the raid I thought it wasn't going to work. However, I gave the fighters their last orders: 'You should see the raid at any moment now. They're at two o'clock, only four miles away.' Then the Y unit rang up to say: 'Eureka! The Italians have jettisoned their bombs and the German 109 leader is telling the Stuka captain what he thinks of him.' Which was rather interesting.

Although the bulk of the Desert Air Force's work was in direct support of the Army, some of the medium bomber squadrons were engaged in more long-range activities. The journalist Edward Ward accompanied one bomber crew during a night raid over Benghazi in September 1941:

We took off for Benghazi along a flare path. I dozed in the back of the plane until we were about half an hour away from our objective. We kept a look out for night fighters but it was a very dark night and we saw nothing. As we approached the target the wireless operator lifted the heavy parachute flares out of their racks and placed them ready alongside the trap from which they were to be dropped.

Everything was deathly still as we passed over Benghazi, except, of course, for the roar of our engines. Then a flare lit up the whole place – one of the other planes had got there before us. Almost instantly, the whole sky was pierced with a ring of searchlights which crisscrossed each other like a spider's web. We flew in over the target and dropped a flare ourselves, then flew out and circled round to find our target. I could hear the orders being given on my headphones: 'We're just coming up to it. A litle bit to the left. Now!' And the observer released our first stick of bombs.

We didn't get a chance to see where they landed, however. I was standing up in the middle of the plane watching through the dome blister. Suddenly the whole aircraft was floodlit. We had got caught by a searchlight. Soon every searchlight in the place was on us. Then all the guns started firing up at us. The pilot said to me later: 'When they catch you like that they put up everything they know, even the breech blocks of the guns!'

Most of the shells were exploding underneath us with nasty thumps which several times knocked me off my feet. One exploded right under the tail and the plane gave a sickening lurch. For a moment, the pilot and I thought we had been hit. All the time we were dodging in an attempt to get away from these maddening searchlights. Finally the pilot put the bomber into a fast shallow dive and we made our escape.

We then circled round again and approached the target once more. A great sheet of flame shot up from alongside the outer mole of the harbour. One of the planes had scored a direct hit on a ship in the harbour. We turned out again in order to approach the target from another direction. As we drew near the flames from the ship spluttered out – it must have sunk. The searchlights came on together making a network which we had to go through to get to the target. I don't know how we managed to make it through those beams without being picked up again. But we did and we dropped our last stick of bombs and then turned back and made for home.

As in Europe daylight bomber raids without fighter escort could be suicidal against a well-prepared enemy. Flight Lieutenant Wallace par-

A game of draughts passes the time for RAF pilots as they wait for the order to scramble. Such scenes were common to all theatres of war, where fighter pilots were forced to spend hours hanging around in dispersal for the call to action. (CM.1254)

ticipated in one such raid against a German airfield in Tunisia on 4 December 1942:

We had been at our forward aerodrome all morning and were feeling pretty brassed off because there was nothing to do. All week we'd been co-operating with the Army, out bombing tanks and shooting up transport. But this particular morning was a blank.

Then, just about lunchtime, the orderly chap came running out with a signal: an order to go out and bomb an enemy fighter airfield. That's a tough proposition at any time but when the CO, Wing Commander Malcolm, said there wouldn't be any fighter cover for us – there wasn't time to arrange it – well, we all knew what that meant. It was a fine, sunny day with not a cloud in the sky. The Hun were certain to see us coming and we knew there'd be a fighter patrol over the airfield – there always was. But Malcolm was a superb leader and all of us would have followed him anywhere.

We clambered into our machines and took off. As we climbed I remember doing all the routine things, like spreading out my map, giving the gun sights a polish and through the screen I could just see Malcolm's plane leading.

As we got nearer the target I put on my tin hat. I know it sounds silly but somehow it made me feel better. We saw the formation tighten. The Huns were on to us and there were shells bursting all round. By this time we'd reached the range of hills between us and the target. My hand was on the bomb switch

waiting until we were dead on the spot. From the bomb aiming position I could see bursts of cannon fire chasing us along the ground but they never touched us.

Then, bombs were bursting right across the airfield – ours included. As we turned sharply away I had my first chance to look up: the sky was black with aircraft – Messerschmitt 109Fs – there must have been fifty or sixty of them and only ten of our planes. The one on my left was on fire, but I didn't have much time to look on it. A Messerschmitt was coming on our starboard quarter. We'd got separated from the rest of the formation somehow. But I was too busy firing at the Hun to worry about that.

We were weaving up the valleys between the hills and they made about six attacks on us. I thought we'd had it. The intercom went dead and a moment or two later the starboard engine caught fire. I was trying to climb out of the cockpit when we hit the ground with a colossal whoomph!

Flames ran through the cockpit like a red wind. It was incredible that any of us got out at all. I wrenched off my helmet and slid down the side of the fuselage. Somehow the pilot and the gunner got out and we met by the side of the crackling, burning wreck. The pilot asked where we were. I said 'No Man's Land', and we began to run in the direction we'd been flying.

Raising clouds of dust, a Boston bomber of the South African Air Force takes off on a raid. Manufactured in America as the Douglas DB-7 the Boston suffered a series of teething troubles when it arrived in the desert but after extensive modification it went on to become an effective medium bomber. (CM.2903)

The Messerschmitts were still overhead as we started up the hill. It was rough, stony ground and I felt like death. I don't think the others were much better either. Then we saw men running down the hill towards us. I glanced round to have a look at our plane and there were more men chasing us up the hill. We couldn't tell who was who. Then we saw the men who were coming down towards us were wearing British tin hats. It seemed a hell of a time before they reached us. Then one of them shouted: 'Are you all right?' I remember saying yes, then I passed out. That was the end of the raid as far as I was concerned, but we'd done what we'd set out to do – wreck the Hun airfield.

Wing Commander Malcolm was killed on the raid but for his courageous leadership in this and other missions he was awarded a posthumous Victoria Cross.

A last quotation comes from Frederick Rosier, summing up the air war in North Africa:

I thought the desert was fascinating. It was in the desert that we developed ways of supporting the Army, which stood us in good stead for the rest of the war. In fact, all the support work for the Normandy invasion and afterwards was based on what we had done in the desert.

PART SIX

DESERT VICTORY

*'The click of a rifle bolt sounded a
few yards in front. It acted like a signal.
The patrol hurled grenades and attacked.
One of our corporals was killed as he
stood up, and a private was shot in the
foot. The remainder rushed in, passed a
machine-gun post and found a German
shamming dead'.*
J. R. OATES, *No. 5 Field Unit*

Alamein and After

On 3 August 1942 the British Prime Minister Winston Churchill arrived in Egypt to attend the Cairo Conference and to see for himself how the Eighth Army was faring. Churchill was not happy with what he saw. The failures of the summer and what he considered as Auchinleck's continuing intransigence meant a change at the top was inevitable.

On 6 August General Sir Harold Alexander was chosen to replace Auchinleck as Commander-in-Chief and command of the Eighth Army was given to Lieutenant-General W. H. E. Gott. Before he could take up the appointment, however, Gott was killed when the transport aircraft he was travelling in was shot down by German fighters. His replacement was Lieutenant-General B. L. Montgomery. Brought out from England, Montgomery was a highly abrasive individual who had little time for the 'bad old ways' of the desert generals – either they would conform to his way of doing things or they would go.

Before Montgomery could impose his stamp on the Eighth Army he was called upon to defend the Alamein position against the last-gasp attack of the Afrika Korps. In an operation subsequently known as the battle of Alam Halfa, Rommel followed the well-tried formula of a wide, swinging attack around the British southern flank with his armoured

The newly arrived commander of the Eighth Army, Lieutenant-General Bernard Montgomery (pointing centre), surveys the tactical situation with officers from the 22nd Armoured Brigade on 20 August 1942, shortly before the battle of Alam Halfa. Lieutenant-General Brian Horrocks, commander of XIII Corps, is standing third from left. (E.15788)

formations. The British defensive plan, based on that proposed by Auchinleck and his deputy chief of staff, Major-General Eric Dorman-Smith, anticipated the German move.

The Axis forces were allowed to make their flanking attack on 30/31 August but were funnelled towards strong British positions on the Alam Halfa ridge. As they made their advance the Axis formations were harassed by heavy RAF bomber attacks while shortages of petrol further slowed their rate of progress. Determined British resistance along the Alam Halfa Ridge brought the Axis offensive to a standstill. Rommel's armour was now in a vulnerable position and prudently he ordered a retreat. By 6 September the Axis forces was back on their start line.

As usual Churchill pressed for an immediate resumption of offensive operations but Montgomery refused to be rushed. Ever the methodical planner, Montgomery set about building up morale and training his troops for the next battle, which he believed would seal the fate of the campaign in North Africa.

Montgomery made great play of the poor morale of the Eighth Army on his arrival and his disparaging and inaccurate comments on Auchinleck's tenure of Eighth Army command reflected badly on Montgomery himself. None the less the army needed shaking up and Montgomery was certainly the man for that. Despite their obvious partisan bias, Montgomery's own views (taken from his 'Review of the Situation of the Eighth Army from 12 August 1942 to 23 October 1942') are of considerable interest:

Gross mismanagement, faulty command and bad staff work had been the cause of the whole thing. But the final blame must rest on General Auchinleck for allowing an inexperienced general like Ritchie to mishandle grossly a fine fighting army, and for allowing a policy of dispersion to rule.

Even allowing for an element of exaggeration – and a complete absence of credit for Auchinleck's sure tactical handling during the Crusader and First Alamein battles – there was some truth in Montgomery's accusations. On other aspects of the Eighth Army's performance he was equally severe:

I was watching the training very carefully, and it was becoming apparent that the Eighth Army was very untrained. The need for training had never been stressed; consequently no one ever did any training; most of the officers had come to the fore by skill in battle and because there was no one any better who could be promoted; these officers were not skilled trainers.

There were very few really first-class officers in the Middle East in the higher ranks; most of the No. One jobs were filled by second- and third-rate officers. Here again Auchinleck was to blame; he continually refused to have good men sent out from England, preferring the second-rate man on the spot whom he knew.

Montgomery's skill for self-publicity soon had its effect on the troops. He made endless trips to the units under his command as part of his mission to build up a new Eighth Army spirit. His behaviour elicited mixed feelings from the men but on the whole they were favourable. Harold Harper saw Montgomery several times and was impressed: 'For

An explosion throws sand up into the sky as a gun crew shelters beside a 6-pounder anti-tank gun on the edge of the Qattara Depression, 3 September 1942. Although the battle of Alam Halfa was fought to the north of this position both British and Germans engaged in constant rounds of artillery duelling in the southernmost part of the Alamein line. (E.16406)

the first time in the war we had a commander who told us man-for-man what was happening. It was all very encouraging. He would talk on the same level as the men. He gained great respect from me.'

The idea of giving more information to the troops was extended down the chain of command, at least in Louis Challoner's battery of the RHA where junior officers began to discuss matters with the men:

Mr Stephenson made it his habit to come round daily with the fighting map and explain to us the current position. What a difference this makes to morale only a gunner can tell; yet it should be obvious to the meanest intelligence that when men are ordered to fight without any explanation at all, they soon lose all interest and begin to think that war is just a game the higher-ups play.

Montgomery had decided that his great offensive would open on the night of 23 October. During the seven weeks at his disposal from the end of the battle of Alam Halfa until then he set about building up his forces and rehearsing his men in battle craft. Patrols and small probing operations were a feature of this period, intended for the most part to gain information of enemy positions. In the Australian sector patrols developed into a way of life, according to J. R. Oates of No. 5 Field Unit:

These nightly forays into No Man's Land, and on many occasions into German occupied territory itself, yielded good results. Not only were casualties inflicted

on the enemy and information gained, but in many cases weapons and stores were captured. Working on information gleaned by patrols, parties of engineers made a feature of penetrating the enemy lines, stealing dumps of mines, and sowing them in enemy territory.

At first our patrols were very successful, but the Germans soon began to wire themselves in, bringing up more machine-guns, mines and booby traps. These counter-measures and the increasing strength of the moon made the work of patrols more hazardous. Although lacking many of the more spectacular successes of the earlier period, they nevertheless continued to harry the enemy, wearing his nerves and, by being an ever-present potential menace, preventing him from using men and material for reinforcing other sectors.

An outstanding patrol in the early period was carried out on the night of 4/5 August. Composed of an officer, two NCOs and ten men, the patrol made for the German wire. On being challenged they moved forward for 180 yards, when they were once again challenged. Realizing that they were surrounded by Germans in dug-in positions, the Australians went to ground, placing Brens on each flank.

The click of a rifle bolt sounded a few yards in front. It acted like a signal. The patrol hurled grenades and attacked. One of our corporals was killed as he stood up, and a private was shot in the foot. The remainder rushed in, passed a machine-gun post and found a German shamming dead. The captain in charge and a corporal dragged him to his feet. Not far away another member of the

An Australian YMCA van comes under fire while visiting the front line, September 1942. These vans would regularly come up to the front to supply troops in the trenches with cigarettes, sweets and prodigious quantities of tea and coffee. (E.17230)

patrol had killed three Germans in a pit, and then jumped into it with a Tommy gun. By this time the enemy had opened fire all round. The German prisoner was shot through the chest and killed, and the captain wounded. He quickly searched the dead German, taking documents and identification markings, but on being wounded again, he lost consciousness. He was carried out by a corporal who took command of the patrol and organized the withdrawal. The captain later regained consciousness and walked the rest of the distance to his company headquarters.

As well as patrolling, the Eighth Army initiated a number of local attacks designed to test the Axis positions and provide better jumping-off points for the main battle. In the north the Australian raid (Operation Bulimba) was a partial success but a larger action further south was a resounding failure. Designed to clear the Munasib Depression, Operation Braganza involved 131 Brigade of the 44th Infantry Division. Ernest Norris was a soldier in one of three battalions from the Queen's Own Regiment that made up 131 Brigade. He describes how getting lost on the approach march made them late for the start:

I don't know by how much but we were certainly delayed. The creeping barrage was too far in front of us but we couldn't change that. We fixed bayonets, formed up in line and were given the order, 'Forward'. At the time I felt pretty good, proud even. Our barrage was going on ahead and it gave us a feeling of protection. Then suddenly the barrage stopped; you feel so naked you can't describe it.

In a matter of a seconds they were firing tracer bullets at us. It was still dark and I was aware of the tracer coming towards us – they seemed too slow to be bullets. But there were men getting killed and wounded all around. Captain Clarke was mortally wounded and I heard him call out. 'Carry on, Mr Cole-Biroth. I've been hit.' Then my Bren gunner screamed and went down. I mentally panicked. You don't know what's happening. By then it was almost daylight. We got down behind what cover we could find. I looked round: Captain Clarke was dead, Mr Cole-Biroth was pretty badly wounded and Mr Whittacker had most of his face shot away. We had no officers left.

We were so close to the enemy that they could see us clearly and they began mortaring us. And as we'd gone past enemy machine-gun posts in our advance we were being fired at from behind as well as in front. We couldn't move forwards or backwards but we tried to reply to their fire as best we could. Eventually we heard voices and we knew the enemy were coming for us. Then we saw them standing above us and making signs to throw our rifles down and come out. And that's what we did.

Lieutenant-Colonel J. Anderson Smith was an anti-tank specialist assigned to the 44th Division. He observed the abortive attack from the Divisional HQ:

Things hadn't gone quite according to plan. Opposition was considerably more than expected, the Queen's had a lot of casualties and one company had surrendered more or less complete. The Brigadier [E. H. C. Frith of 131 Brigade] was looking pretty glum and was having rather a hard time trying to conduct the battle with both the corps commander Horrocks (Lieutenant-General Brian Horrocks] and the divisional commander Hughes (Major-

South African sappers practise their mine-sweeping skills using a mechanical detector. In the period leading up to the main battle of Alamein, tens of thousands of mines had been laid in front of the Axis positions and if the British attack was not to be bogged down in these minefields it was essential that they be cleared swiftly and thoroughly. (E.18844)

General I. T. P. Hughcs] looking over his shoulder. He was replaced soon after this. I don't know if he was any good but I never felt he had much chance there.

As well as the information brought in by constant patrolling, Eighth Army intelligence used straightforward observation from ground and air to map out the position of the Axis defences. A member of a South African field survey company, V. L. Bosazza, explains his work in the weeks leading up to the battle of Alamein:

In September our artillery drew attention to the fact that the Axis guns, particularly their 88s, either did not have alternate positions or did not use them. A British survey company officer came up and helped us with unmarked triangulation stations far forward. At the same time four tubular scaffolding towers were erected to observe enemy positions. With help from aerial photographs we gradually built up an accurate plot of the order of battle of almost the entire enemy artillery. When we went forward after the battle I especially visited the 88mm gun sites and there were dead around each gun, hit by our 5.5in medium guns on the night of 23/24 October.

The commander of the 51st (Highland) Division, Major-General Douglas Wimberley was told by Montgomery on 15 September that his troops would be part of the main assault force. A disciple of the Montgomery school of warfare he initiated a rigorous training programme:

We were in a fortunate position, only a small proportion of our fighting troops were in the line at one time with the Australians, and we were able to give our troops preparatory training for the forthcoming battle. I was allotted an area of open desert and here with the aid of sappers I laid out an exact replica of the enemy defences. Then I took my men, a brigade at a time, and practised every battalion in the exact job it was to do in the initial attack..

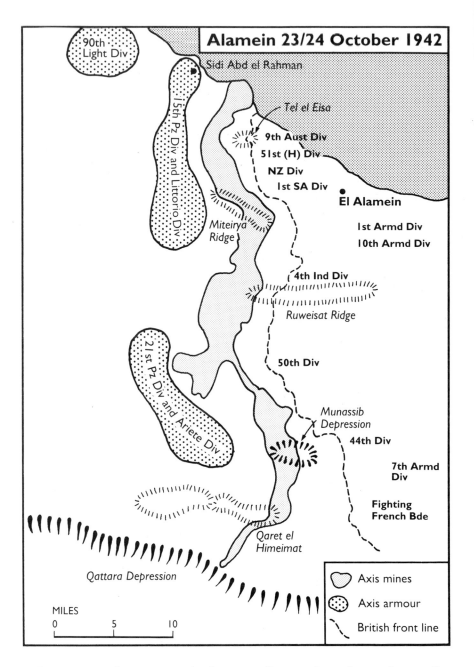

Alamein 23/24 October 1942

90th Light Div

Sidi Abd el Rahman

Tel el Eisa

9th Aust Div

51st (H) Div

15th Pz Div and Littorio Div

NZ Div

1st SA Div

El Alamein

1st Armd Div

10th Armd Div

Miteirya Ridge

4th Ind Div

Ruweisat Ridge

50th Div

21st Pz Div and Ariete Div

Munassib Depression

44th Div

7th Armd Div

Fighting French Bde

Qaret el Himeimat

Qattara Depression

MILES
0   5   10

⬭ Axis mines

⬚ Axis armour

- - - British front line

Dummy trenches were made the exact distance from the mock start line based on maps and air photos. Then I used the divisional artillery to fire the same barrage they would fire in the battle, at the same rate and with the same pauses for leap frogging. Meanwhile the divisional signals carried out the same outline plan, reporting the capture of objectives; and the sappers did their clearing of mines through dummy minefields.

Amongst other preparations we constructed a large sand model of the posts we were to take. I went over the initial attack very carefully on the model with all the officers – regimental and staff – down to the rank of lieutenant-colonel.

Remembering how hopeless one felt without communications, I decided that wireless or no wireless I would lay down as much telephone cable as I could – and bury it too! For that reason and also because I wanted to show that I had complete confidence that the Jocks would take their objectives, I decided to dig in my battle HQ practically in the British front line. I was consequently well placed to control the battle on 24 October and didn't have to waste hours on dusty tracks going back to Divisional HQ.

While the British continued to prepare for the attack, the Axis forces improved their defences, the Germans 'corsetting' the Italian infantry in the front line with their own infantry units while keeping their armoured formations back in two reserve positions. Worn out and ill, Rommel had left Africa to recuperate in Germany, leaving command in the hands of General Georg Stumme.

For the first time in the Desert War, the British had a clear numerical and material advantage over the Axis: 195,000 men against 104,000 (50,000 German); 1029 tanks against 489 (211 German); 2311 guns of all types against 1219 (644 German); and 530 serviceable aircraft against 350 (150 German).

Montgomery's plan maximized his resources. As the Axis line, running from the Mediterranean coast to the impassable Qattara Depression, could not be turned by a flanking manoeuvre, Montgomery decided to attack frontally in the north. An attritional battle of this kind played to British military strengths while reducing the advantages of mobility possessed by the panzer divisions.

The Eighth Army was divided into three corps. XXX Corps (Lieutenant-General Oliver Leese) contained the main strike force of 9th Australian, 51st (Highland), New Zealand and 1st South African Divisions, which would smash their way through the enemy line. Two corridors were to be opened up in the Axis minefields through which would drive the armoured divisions of X Corps (Lieutenant-General Herbert Lumsden). Instead of attempting an immediate breakout X Corps would take up defensive positions with the infantry of XXX Corps to await and wear down the inevitable counter-attack from the Axis armoured divisions. To the south XIII Corps (Lieutenant-General Brian Horrocks) was to launch two subsidiary attacks to tie down enemy forces in that area during the highly critical first phase of the battle.

Although the fact of the British offensive could not be kept hidden, its time and precise location were successfully concealed from the Germans. On 23 October, the Eighth Army silently took up its battle positions. General Wimberley recalls the opening of the attack:

As we motored forward it was amazingly quiet. Hardly a gun or shell broke the silence. In fact, with memories of the 1914–18 War, I thought it was really too quiet to be true. One thousands guns were to start firing at 2140 hours, and in the stillness that preceded the storm I stood at one of the gaps in the wire and watched my Jocks in the moonlight. Platoon by platoon they filed past, heavily laden with pick and shovel, sandbags and grenades – the officer at the head, his piper by his side. There was nothing more that I could do now to prepare for the battle, it was only possible to pray for their success, and that the Highland Division would live up to its name and the names of those very famous regiments of which it was composed.

The great Alamein artillery barrage, evening of 23 October 1942. This photograph was taken near the British front line looking rearwards to the gun line several thousand yards behind. The vehicles silhouetted on the horizon are ambulances and troop carriers waiting for the infantry attack to go in as the barrage lifts. (E.18465)

I went back to my battle post and ate a little food, and when the guns behind us opened up with a roar, we went on the roof to hear the shells swishing over our heads as they sped towards the German batteries. I had done the same at Passchaendale as a young captain in September 1917, twenty-five years before. Now came the long wait, as at 10pm my Jocks on their six-battalion frontage went into the attack.

The massive British artillery barrage – the biggest in the Desert War – was an experience few forgot. The veteran tankman Bob Sykes remembered it vividly:

We sat talking until it became dark, a few outbreaks of firing here and there and then absolutely dead quiet. Suddenly, way up north a searchlight lit up, pointing straight up, followed by another. Then the night sky lit up with the biggest gun barrage I have ever known. The noise was more than deafening; everything seemed to go round and round.

Harold Harper's South Notts Hussars, reformed after its destruction at Knightsbridge back in June, had been rearmed with 5.5-inch guns. A sergeant-major in charge of a gun team, Harper recalls his experiences of the bombardment:

It was beyond description. Nothing had been seen like it before, or after. The entire lot started firing at the precise second and the whole sky seemed to burst. After firing ten or twelve rounds I suddenly thought, 'Blimey, this is beginning to get hard work!' Then I noticed that one bloke was missing, hiding in a split

Above: The crew of a cruiser tank attempt to see how the artillery–infantry battle is progressing, 23/24 October 1942. This photograph and the one opposite were taken by Sergeant Stanley Gladstone – *see* page 183. (E.18478)

Left: A piper entertains troops of the Highland Division during a lull in the fighting. In Highland regiments the bagpipes were considered to be weapons of war, a vital element in sustaining morale. (E.18732)

trench behind the gun. So I dragged him out by the scruff of the neck in the middle of the barrage. I threatened to shoot him if he didn't get back on the job. I had to do something drastic because if you do get that sort of thing in action and do nothing it becomes contagious.

I would have shot him if I had to. I know it sounds terrible now but we were a different sort of animal in those days. He went back to the gun but was never quite the same again.

At his forward HQ Wimberley anxiously waited upon the news of his troops' progress. After initial reports that enemy shelling was relatively light he received this information:

I got the code-word 'Inverness'. It was the first of many to come in that night and it did my heart good: Ian Davy with his Camerons had taken their first objective. Hour by hour the code-words came in, and by dawn it was clear to me that we had eaten deeply into the enemy's position. Casualties might well have been worse.

In the midst of the fighting was Sergeant Covell of the Gordon Highlanders. He provided this account – for a BBC sound recording – of the first phase of the battle:

At about 7 o'clock that night we collected all our equipment and moved up to the start line. All you could hear was the sound of people laughing and talking all around us. Everyone was in very high spirits and looking forward to getting their own back after the last do in France at St Valery [the 51st (Highland) Division had been cut off at the Channel port of St Valery in 1940, and been forced to surrender to the commander of the 7th Panzer Division – Erwin Rommel].

When the Black Watch moved forward we followed and then went through them. There was a lot of opposition from machine-gun posts, but we soon mopped them up with bayonet and grenades. We took our objectives and held onto them like grim death until the tanks came through.

By dawn of 24 October the infantry had gained most of their objectives but there was an immediate problem getting the tanks up. Determined enemy resistance combined with congestion along the routes through the minefields prevented a proper deployment of the armoured formations. After the initial shock of the Eighth Army attack, Axis resistance stiffened. From now on the battle settled down into a slugging match.

Sergeant 'Scuttler' Maile was a tank commander in one of the leading elements of the British armoured attack on 23/24 October. After being held up crossing a partially cleared minefield the British tanks clambered up a ridge where they came under heavy and accurate enemy fire:

Coming up to the ridge we were all alone. We were right out in front, one tank burning on the left, one tank burning on the right. We were being hit with high explosive (HE) and anti-tank rounds. The enemy guns had us at pretty close range and we were right up there on the skyline.

We'd only just got there when I looked over the side and saw that one of our caterpillar tracks was off; we couldn't move now. The bow gunner was the first to notice the enemy gun facing us. He shouted: 'Look! There's a bloody big bus over there, pointed straight at us.' Then we saw it in an emplacement only 200

yards away. We got our gun on it. Everybody was jumping about. We hit him square but as we hit him he hit us. There was a sudden shock and flames burst out under us. I gave the order to bale out and we threw ourselves down in the sand.

I could see that only two tanks had made the ridge, our officer's and mine. And they'd both gone up in smoke. We joined up with their crew. There were nine of us altogether. We were lying there in the sand being plastered with HE, some of it from our own barrage We had one shell drop ten yards to the left of us, another in front. We were all very close, lying flat. I was trying to scoop just a little sand out of the ground to hide myself – pressing my face down in it. You didn't dare move a muscle.

The mutilated body of a German tank crewman lies beside his knocked-out tank. The battle had settled into a struggle of attrition. (E.16495)

Above and opposite: A sequence of two photographs showing a British advance towards a ridge and the troops diving for cover as they come under Axis artillery fire. (E.18805/18807)

About half an hour later we saw a Jerry patrol come out to fetch us in. They had bayonets and there were about fifty of them and only nine of us. It was devilishly thick with heavy explosions and we could see the Jerries falling as they were coming up. We hadn't anything to fire with, of course. We were just waiting for someone to hit us. It was especially bad for those who were in it for the first time.

The officer was talking to us when he was hit in the back of the neck and killed. The fellow on the left, my driver, got a bit of shrapnel in his ear. He said he was feeling faint and I said: 'Don't be stupid. Wait until your head's blown off!' That was the way to keep their morale up.

The enemy infantry had been turned back by the barrage, but they sniped at us every time we tried to move. They knew exactly where we were. We tried to dig ourselves further in, with our bare hands, but we had to give it up because they shot at us. We'd been there three and a half hours, waiting for darkness. But the moon spoiled that.

The Jerries came for us again when it was dark. We could see their bayonets gleaming. I don't know whether they thought we had machine-guns but they came round very carefully. Our line of retreat was between the blazing tanks. And they took up a position so that if we ran we would be silhouetted in front of the two tanks and they could shoot us.

I'd taken over command after the officer was killed and I told them there were only two options, and I certainly wasn't going to surrender. Everyone said: 'We'll do what you're going to do.' They were very cheerful about it, although

some were pretty badly wounded. I remember one fellow had to keep his arms up because he had cuts all over them that were bleeding and burnt. He couldn't do anything else. He said to me ruefully: 'It looks as though I am ruddy well surrendering now.'

We had only a short distance to go to get back to our own chaps. It was our only chance to get through, so we made our dash between the two blazing tanks and somehow made it without loss. We had been given up for lost, although after a tank engagement people drift back in ones and twos. Because I was always getting shot out of tanks, I was called Scuttler. I had lost seven but got twenty-two German tanks in exchange. The next day we moved on to the same ridge with a new tank and we could see the hulks of all our knocked-out tanks.

General Stumme had died of a heart attack on the opening of the British attack but with the sudden return of Rommel on 25 October German counter-attacks increased in ferocity. Montgomery was forced to bring up reinforcements from XIII Corps in the south (their own diversionary attacks had come to nothing) in order to carry out his tactical ploy of 'crumbling' the enemy line. The 7th Battalion, the Rifle Brigade, was part of 7th Motor Brigade, now deployed between the Australian and Highland Divisions. D. A. Main, a sergeant in 7th Rifle Brigade, found himself repelling a German attack:

About 2.30pm, approximately thirty tanks appeared in front of us, consisting of a few German Mark IIIs and the remaining Italian M-13s. At the same time a heavy barrage was brought down on our positions, plus machine-gun and mortar fire. Since we were in the front with our machine-guns, as the tanks drew closer we had to stop firing and take cover in our slit trenches. Events now moved rapidly. Our sixteen six-pounders engaged the tanks, several firing at one particular tank, so that the closest was knocked out fifty yards in front. The Battalion was credited with fourteen tanks.

As some of the enemy tanks were hit, the occupants tired to escape through the turrets. One Italian officer was hoisting himself out when a six-pounder shot hit him in the chest and he literally disintegrated. In front of the stationary tanks were two Italians sitting on the ground.

From the right came cries of 'You rotten Pommie bastards!' The Australians strongly objected to our knocking out the tanks with our six-pounders before they came within range of their two-pounders. Finally, as the barrage had now died down, my platoon commander suggested a bayonet counter-attack. As there was no future in this I asked him if he had a touch of the sun.

After sunset a Highland Division attack was launched on our left in the moonlight. We heard their pipers and then all hell was let loose as enemy concentrations of shellfire were put down. The sky was lit by a burning 15cwt truck and the attack failed.

When the tank attack had been halted and the shelling had ceased, I heard my left machine-gun fire a burst, and one of the two wounded Italians was killed. I found that the rifleman responsible was surprisingly a member of the Plymouth Brethren. He told me that he thought he would put the Italian out of his misery. I told him not to fire again without orders. As the shelling had died down I then went to the remaining Italian and carried him to my slit trench. He had been wounded in the thigh and after I had put a shell dressing on his wound, he proceeded to kiss me, so I had him evacuated by the stretcher-bearers as soon as possible.

Behind the slight rising ground, we could hear in front of us the noise of tank tracks moving. My morale was not particularly high in view of the fact that if we were again attacked by tanks we were to allow them to run over our positions, and then to engage the enemy infantry.

Next morning there had been no further tank attacks but we immediately found that the Germans had put snipers in the knocked-out tanks. My range taker, Gerry Sayer, was now suffering from shell-shock and whenever I took his instrument to see what was going on in front of us, he would try to stop me saying 'You'll be killed!' Behind me Rifleman Rogers was very severely shell-shocked and we tied him to a stretcher with an old machine-gun belt and put a pencil between his teeth. Two stretcher bearers then took him to the rear.

Until we were relieved by the Highland Division the snipers and mortar fire accounted for half the platoon. We now made our way to the remaining trucks and were taken to the rear, to obtain replacement vehicles and reinforcements. During the last four days and nights in action I had had about two hours' sleep, and when I found a small piece of mirror to shave I was startled to see wild eyes and cordite marks on my face.

The 2nd Battalion, the Rifle Brigade was another 7th Motor Brigade unit sent forward to absorb the storm of the German attacks. Major-General Raymond Briggs, commander of the 1st Armoured Division (containing 7th Motor Brigade), remembers the battalion's defence of a small rise known as Snipe Ridge:

Above: Major Tom Bird MC and bar, the commander of the anti-tank company which did such damage to Axis armour on Snipe Ridge.

Above left: Major-General R. Briggs (left) GOC of 1st Armoured Division, talks to Brigadier E.C.N. Custance, commander of 8th Armoured Brigade.

The first counter-attack came in at 3am on the 27th and between then and dusk no less than eight major attacks were directed on the unfortunate but by no means unhappy battalion. Withholding the fire of their twelve six-pounder anti-tank guns until the enemy tanks were frequently within 150 yards range they did terrific damage.

In the meantime I was listening on my headphones at my tactical headquarters (on the other side of a valley) to the course of the battle and to the appeals for tank assistance. I gave orders directing the tanks to their aid but every move across the valley was met by intense anti-tank fire and the loss of my tanks.

There was another factor too, known only to me and which I could not disclose. News had just reached me that the 21st Panzer Division was on the move from the south to join the 15th Panzer Division opposing us. I knew that every tank would be needed at short notice, as indeed they were a few hours later, to take on the two divisions. I had to balance the possible destruction of the Rifle Brigade against the necessity to conserve my tank state. My reluctant decision was that I must leave the infantrymen to fight it out themselves. How wonderfully that decision was upheld and with what comparatively little loss of life.

The CO, Colonel Vic Turner, was wounded in the head early in the engagement but refused to give up and carried on by sheer guts almost until the end. His award of a Victoria Cross was described by Field Marshal Alexander, 'as one of the finest of the war'. After the battle I had an independent survey made of the tanks and guns still lying around the position. In the few hours of the fighting that unit had brewed up thirty-five tanks and damaged beyond repair another twenty.

Although the German counter-attacks were being held by the Eighth Army, the British were unable to make progress and casualties were beginning to mount up. Montgomery decided to call a temporary halt to

A 25-pounder gun engages
Axis anti-tank positions
which had been delaying the
advance of the British
armoured formations through
the narrow gaps in the
minefields. (E.18538)

the offensive and regroup his now rather disorganized forces. In the
north, however, the Australians maintained their offensive, which continued to gain ground, and also drew away valuable German reserves
from other sectors.

The renewed British assault (Operation Supercharge) was launched
in the early hours of 2 November. As with the opening attack, operations
were preceded by a fearsome bombardment. The journalist Godfrey
Talbot recorded this impressionistic piece:

Up in front where the shells were crashing red, the noise was a diabolical
mixture, with the crackling of small-arms fire and the bursting of mortar
bombs. Flares went up and lit all the sandy, scrubby, hummocky ground; they
burnt very bright and made you feel somehow naked. There was the crisscross
of tracer fire and rocket-like bursts. Through it all sometimes you heard the
drone of aircraft.

Back at the guns there was a moment when the near batteries paused and
save for the more distant rumbling it was almost quiet. It was weird then to hear
the chirp of a bird or cricket. Up at the front the sappers and infantry were at
work, clearing away, fighting grimly against determined opposition.

When we saw the armour moving up it was an almost ghostly sight. Tank
engines roared and tracks squealed as the columns moved forward. Black noisy
shapes in the night, each tank creating a choking fog of dust as it moved
through the sand. You could hardly see them in these clouds until they were
nearly on top of you. And so we saw these strange dramatic glimpses of the
armed might of the Eighth Army moving into battle.

The two brigades (151 and 152) of the 50th Infantry Division were
brought up to provide support for the armoured attack. An officer in the

6th Durham Light Infantry (151 Brigade) W. I. Watson was involved in the attack on the right flank:

At 12.40 everybody stood up, put on their equipment and got their magazines charged. I loaded my revolver and throughout the advance I carried it in my hand. You also heard the click, click, click as the chaps fixed bayonets. At five to one we started to walk slowly forward. In silence we walked through the minefields. I had practically no casualties. At five past one every gun opened up and the shells came screaming over our heads while the Bofors guns started to fire tracer straight ahead to keep direction. I can remember hearing the pipers from the Highlanders and the next day when I was wandering about the battlefield I found a set of pipes and returned it to the regiment.

The barrage thundering over your head was nerve-racking to start with. In the end it became almost a song. There were twenty-two lifts before half-time. Very quickly the whole atmosphere was smoke, sand and mist. Then we saw figures with their arms up looming out of the mist – Germans and Italians surrendering. After we'd done about 880 yards we received enemy fire from our right which slowed us down a bit. Also we must have walked over some Italians who lay doggo as we advanced and undoubtedly one of them killed my RSM, the doctor tending the wounded and a sergeant who played cricket down in Dorset.

Sergeant Main, of the 7th Rifle Brigade was soon in the thick of the action again:

In the early evening of 1 November we were told that the 7th Motor Brigade would attack at midnight to force a gap for our tanks. When darkness fell I tossed up with my particular friend Sergeant Brine to decide who would split

A Sherman tank moves forward at speed as the Axis defences begin to crumble. Armed with a 75mm main gun, the US-manufactured Sherman first saw extensive action at Alamein and in 1942 was a reasonable match for German armour in Egypt and Libya. (E.19355)

the watch until midnight. I won and slept first. Meanwhile we had sent out a patrol which could only hear enemy rations being distributed and we were unaware whether the enemy positions were Italian or German.

At midnight we fixed bayonets and proceeded in the moonlight towards the Rahman track. D (Lloyd's) Company were leading with two platoons forward and one (mine) immediately behind. All was quiet until we were about fifty yards from the enemy positions, when the Germans opened up enfilade fire from tracer-firing machine-guns on both flanks, together with flares and mortar bombs. The leading left-hand platoon was hit to a man and the right-hand platoon immediately went to ground. I ran forward to get a Bren to fire at the flashes from the enemy machine-guns but it jammed with sand after a couple of bursts.

Above the noise of the explosions I heard the company commander, Major Trappes-Lomax, shout: 'Up the Rifle Brigade! Charge!' Trappes-Lomax disappeared through a hail of tracer bullets. I felt he couldn't go in by himself and I gave the order to charge. I went through the enfilade fire and I couldn't understand how I had not been hit. It was like daylight with the flares and mortar explosions. Sergeant Brine had run straight into a German machine-gun. He was hit all over and before he died he asked to be placed facing the enemy.

I had been advancing in a series of rushes, firing my rifle at the hip. I found myself along with two other riflemen at the rear of the German positions and we heard a German NCO shout: 'English swine right, fire!' Fortunately the machine-gun fired just over our heads as it could not be lowered to fire into the slight depression in which we were lying. From where we lay I could see an 88mm gun at least fifty yards away. I decided to go for this and as I ran with rifle and bayonet, tracer from a German machine-gun was going all around me. However, I considered that if I continued running I would not be hit and eventually reached the gun followed by several riflemen.

We now acquired two German prisoners who had been hiding under a truck. A little later we met up with Major Trappes-Lomax and found that only twenty-two of the Company were left. We now received orders to withdraw. We ran back and I frequently looked over my shoulder to dodge the German tracer fire coming my way. We managed to avoid most of the fire except that a rifleman running alongside me was hit in the side and his right arm shattered. Corporal Sandford and I linked arms with him until we reached a dip in the ground and relative safety. On our return just before daylight a roll-call revealed that D Company had thirteen men left. My platoon consisted of Corporal Sandford, myself and a rifleman who had stayed back because of a scorpion bite.

Rifleman J. G. Harris had noted the vehicle congestion of Operation Supercharge – 'like Piccadilly Circus at rush hour' – which caused problems for the deployment of British armour. Throughout 2 November the British tanks fought a desperate battle against the German panzers; the 9th Armoured Brigade, leading the assault, was badly mauled but the 1st Armoured Division managed to inflict severe casualties on the Axis forces. By the evening of 2 November, Rommel knew he was beaten, his precious armour was exhausted and what tanks he did have up and running were now acutely short of petrol.

During 3 November fighting continued, the Germans just managing

to hold the line on direct orders from Hitler. But further attacks by the 51st and 4th Indian Division ruptured the Axis defences and on 4 November Rommel began his long retreat back towards Tripoli. Montgomery despatched elements of the New Zealand Division and 1st, 7th and 10th Armoured Divisions in pursuit. The follow-up was cautious, however, and Rommel was able to make good his escape. Those Axis forces without motor transport (mainly Italian) fell into allied hands within a matter of days. Major Bob Crisp was engaged in the attempt to trap the 90th Light Division:

The most exciting moment of the battle was when we first cut the coast road in an effort to head off the 90th Light Division. Long columns of Italian and German transport were still swarming along the road westward. My tank was first on to the road, being in the recce squadron. It really came as a tremendous surprise to the enemy when they heard the rattle of our machine-guns.

They put in one attack only with about twenty tanks, but of these only two managed to break through, the rest were destroyed. We collected a tremendous bag of prisoners, tanks, lorries and transport of all kinds.

Montgomery had won a major victory. The Axis forces suffered around 20,000 men killed or wounded and a further 30,000 were captured. The Eighth Army's casualties numbered 13,500. The victory was transformed into a decisive one on 8 November with the news of Operation Torch, the Allied landings in Morocco and Algeria. Rommel was now

A dramatic night-time shot of a Daimler armoured car engaging an enemy target during the advance on Tripoli. Capable of firing only solid shot, its 2-pounder gun had a limited capability when acting in support of infantry operations, as here. Otherwise the Daimler proved a useful reconnaissance vehicle. (E.21334)

EIGHTH ARMY

Personal Message from the Army Commander

To be read out to All Troops

1. The leading units of Eighth Army are now only about 200 miles from TRIPOLI. The enemy is between us and that port, hoping to hold us off.

2. THE EIGHTH ARMY IS GOING TO TRIPOLI.

3. Tripoli is the only town in the Italian Empire overseas still remaining in their possession. Therefore we will take it from them; they will then have no overseas Empire.

The enemy will try to stop us. But if each one of us, whether front-line soldier, or officer or man whose duty is performed in some other sphere, puts his whole heart and soul into this next contest — then nothing can stop us.

Nothing has stopped us since the battle of Egypt began on 23rd October, 1942. Nothing will stop us now.

Some must stay back to begin with, but we will all be in the hunt eventually.

4. ON TO TRIPOLI!

Our families and friends in the home country will be thrilled when they hear we have captured that place.

B. L. Montgomery,

12th January, 1943.   General, G.O.C.-in-C., Eighth Army.

faced with a war on two fronts. No longer could he turn back on the Eighth Army for another round of the Benghazi stakes. He had no option but to fall back on Tunisia where Hitler was belatedly sending him reinforcements.

As Rommel fell back through Libya he made sure that the Eighth Army did not have an easy run. Rearguard actions were fought to slow the British advance while booby traps proved to be a sometimes fatal nuisance. Sergeant Robert Hill of the 1/6th Battalion, Queen's Royal Regiment won a Military Medal during an engagement on the outskirts of Benghazi, when he led a reconnaissance patrol of two Bren carriers to locate enemy positions:

I was in the lead Bren-gun carrier. As we advanced everything was so quiet it seemed unnatural. Then all of a sudden artillery opened up. The second carrier was hit, so we picked up the crew, one of whom was wounded. We carried on advancing at a faster speed and found out where the enemy were. In doing so we came to a wadi and as we got to the lip we spotted an enemy machine-gun nest. The corporal alongside me popped a hand grenade into the nest, getting rid of that one. We turned to our left flank and carried along the lip of the wadi and wiped out four more machine-gun positions and captured four prisoners

Above: Aboard Valentine tanks British troops make their triumphant entry into Tripoli. George Ramsay of the Gordon Highlanders pipes the tanks through the streets of Libya's capital. (E.21591)

Opposite: Written in Montgomery's characteristically confident manner this message signalled the end of the Eighth Army's epic struggle for mastery of the desert. Although the war was to go on in North Africa until May 1943, for the desert veterans Tripoli had always been the goal – and it was now within reach. (E.21325)

before returning to our lines. The chap who was wounded died on the way back.

Kenneth Morris was a clerk in a squadron HQ of the 4th Armoured Brigade, part of the Eighth Army pursuit force:

The Brigade's advance troops entered Benghazi on 20 November. For Brigade HQ the route led inland past Bir Hakeim, cutting off the northern corner of Cyrenaica. On 23 November we sat down for the lunch-time brew and we idly watched two fitters from the signals squadron drive across to a wrecked ambulance to remove mechanical parts for spares. As they threw down their tool kit, the peace was shattered by a booby-trapped mine which exploded under the ambulance wheel. Both men were killed.

The Germans made a stand at El Agheila between 23 November and 13 December but in the face of concerted British pressure they retired into Tripolitania. The British began to face greater resistance from the Germans at Wadi Zemzem and the hilly country around Homs. But again the Germans did not have the resources except to conduct delaying operations.

On 23 January 1943 victorious British troops marched into Tripoli – for years the goal of the Eighth Army. Rommel meanwhile retreated further westward, crossing the Tunisian border on 4 February. He now rallied his forces behind the new defences of the Mareth Line. The fighting would continue in the mountains of Tunisia but for the Eighth Army the war in the deserts of Egypt and Libya was over.

Correspondents and Cameramen

The Second World War was a peoples' war and the military authorities were reluctantly forced to concede that the people must be allowed to know something of what was happening at the front. Each army had its collection of correspondents and cameramen and the Eighth Army had a larger collection than most. Inevitably there was always conflict between the military, who wanted a chronicle of the deeds of their forces and the journalists, who wanted to scratch a bit deeper. Although the newsmen occasionally managed to slip something in, the Army's superior numbers invariably told in the end.

Frank Gillard had flown out to Cairo during the closing stages of the Desert War to be the BBC correspondent at General Headquarters while the other BBC journalist then in North Africa, Godfrey Talbot, followed the troops on the advance towards Tripoli. Gillard explains some of the trials facing a war correspondent:

I found the Cairo job very frustrating indeed. You went to two press conferences a day, at which the official spokesman – nicknamed 'the voice of Cairo' – just handed out whatever news GHQ thought it was good for war reporters to have. You'd no means of checking or confirming it although you did have the advantage in Cairo of having a direct communication with London twice daily.

All the material had to be censored four times over, by the Army, the Navy, the RAF and the Egyptian government. The Egyptian State government was remarkably sensitive about what its commercial short-wave transmitter was saying, especially if one attempted to talk about civil affairs in Egypt. The methods of censorship were extremely crude. Most often the censor just simply took out a pocket knife and if there was something on the record he didn't approve of he just scoured out the particular grooves [recordings were made direct on to disc for later broadcast]. Often he scoured out the grooves behind and in front and by the time the stuff got to London it was very mutilated. In London there was further censorship. There were many channels to go through before your stuff got on air.

Another Cairo-based journalist, Rex Keating, recalls friction with the Public Relations Division:

During the period when the war wasn't going very well, around the time of Rommel's advance to Alamein, there was a sudden stop on correspondents going to the front. They protested and there was a great deal of hard feeling about this. But for reasons the Army didn't let on they just said 'No'. Instead they handed out information which the correspondents had to use to send their despatches. Most followed this line and the information went into the newspapers.

The Australian Broadcasting Company sent the journalist Chester Wilmott (*see also* his report on page 12) to record the voices of the defenders of Tobruk during the 1941 siege. After recording messages from Scottish anti-aircraft gunners he plays back the recording which has been cut directly on to disc. (E.5600)

The BBC radio correspondent Richard Dimbleby was very unhappy about this because he knew it was a bit of a cover-up. He'd got information from good sources that the public was being misled and that they were being told things were much rosier than they were. Dimbleby went to the authorities and told them they were wrong not to tell the full story. At this they forbade him to have anything to do with it and he wasn't allowed to go near the studio.

Dimbleby took the matter right to the top, to Sir Miles Lampson at the British Embassy, and said: 'This is wrong. If you don't let me do it in the usual way I will get the information sent back by other means.' At this Lampson got in touch with the BBC; Dimbleby became a persona non grata and was recalled to England. The BBC wouldn't use him for a time, not until the famous 1000-bomber raid over Germany.

Out in the field the journalists were escorted by conducting officers. Godfrey Talbot remembers his 'minders' with some amusement:

There was a time in the Middle East when half our conducting officers seemed to have been either members of the nobility or at school with the commanders of the armed forces. This had its advantages as they had no problems in getting to see a general: they would just breeze through and I would find myself in front of, perhaps, a corps commander and my conducting officer would say, 'My dear Nigel, how are you, dear boy?' They were much better at their relations with some of the officers we wished to see than reading a map and guiding us along

A journalist working for the BBC knocks out his copy – a description of a visit to a signals unit in the desert – on a portable typewriter, ready for despatch back to Britain. (E.16995)

the desert tracks. I map-read for a number of our conducting officers in those days.

The arrival of Montgomery in July 1942 brought about a change in GHQ's approach to the correspondents. A 'modern' general fully aware of the value of publicity, Montgomery encouraged the journalists to write about the Eighth Army and its commander. Talbot:

Monty was a ball of fire and a great talker. He believed in seeing the people who were concerned with his war, including those who were reporting it. He was very conscious of the BBC and its output. Monty was never one to sit around. He would go out and see the troops, where I would come across him and he would speak to me about how my despatches were going and whether they were getting through.

On one occasion, during the quiet period before Alamein, I wrote in one of my despatches something like: 'the only activity at present is one or two patrols going out'. Monty used to listen to the wireless in his caravan and when he heard this one night he sent out one of his chaps to pull me out of my slit trench to appear before him in his caravan. There he said: 'Talbot, what is this I've just heard? Have the BBC mistreated the messages you send? They seem to think that nothing much is happening here. Now men are dying. Patrols are very active. We are very active. But it seems as though they are saying that the Eighth Army is an idle army. Will you send a message from me to say that this is not the

Winston Churchill – complete with boiler suit and topee – is flanked by General Harold Alexander (left) and Lieutenant-General Montgomery on an inspection of British positions near Alamein, 23 August 1942. (E.15905)

case at all?' To be with Monty was almost to be like a small boy in front of the house master.

Churchill's arrival to view the Alamein position shortly before the battle was eagerly awaited by the war correspondents. Talbot provides this recollection:

Above all the smoke of battle and the actual engagements, I'll always remember Winston Churchill standing on the field of Alamein. Winston was wearing his blue boiler suit and an old sola topee on his head, so frayed he could have worn it at the battle of Omdurman. Winston stood there for a long time, smoking a cigar and carrying a sunshade. He looked like a crumpled old rag bag whereas the generals on either side of him were beautifully dressed in newly dhobied khaki drill.

Monty was talking of course, talking interminably, telling Winston how he was going to knock Rommel for six. In the end Churchill turned and waved Montgomery down and said: 'Montgomery, I shall speak for a moment.' Waving his arm over the expanse of stony plain, he continued: 'This scene is to be the setting of a great conflict of arms and I am very glad to have seen it on the eve of what I know will be a decisive battle.' Off the record Winston also said: 'Alamein is simply miles and miles of austere territory; how Stafford Cripps would like this.'

As the main theatre of war between the end of 1940 and 1942, the

Western Desert attracted camermen as it did correspondents. Along with photographers from the newspapers, the Army Film and Photographic Unit sent stills and cine-film men to record the conflict.

Although the military authorities exercised strict control on the release of photographs and film the camermen were allowed to operate with far greater freedom than the print journalists. Under the command of Captain (later Major) Geoffrey Keating, Army film camermen like Peter Hopkinson were able to roam around to find the right story: 'Nobody said, "You can't do this". Looking back I constantly marvel at the free rein we had. As a combat cameraman you were assigned to a division or brigade but once there you did what you liked.'

Stanley Gladstone, an Army stills cameraman, did find rank a difficulty while working alongside military units in a semi-independent capacity:

At times problems arose because we carried the rank of sergeant. It was often necessary to approach senior officers and this wasn't always acceptable to the military mind, particularly with regular soldiers. In the latter stages of the war, however, and especially after Montgomery's arrival, things improved enormously. He set an example of making us welcome and co-operated whenever possible.

Discipline was relatively loose in the photographic units; the Army accepted that combining spit and polish regulations with the Fleet Street tradition (where many photographers came from) was a lost cause.

A mechanic works on camera repairs in an AFPU mobile workshop in the Western Desert, July 1942. This photograph was taken by Geoffrey Keating who took thousands more during the Desert War, some of which appear in this book – *see*, for example: pages 7, 10, 59 (below), 120 and 186 (below). (E.14929)

183

Gladstone: 'Once one was in and became one of the unit discipline was extremely informal. The units were made up of people who were there to do a professional job. There wasn't much rank consciousness, or of being in the Army.'

William 'Billy' Jordan, a film cameraman, explains how they worked in the field:

We operated using jeeps in two-man teams, one stills the other cine, and were given a mobile and free hand. The only control you had came from the Army Film Unit HQ. We received information on what was happening, where to go and what unit to join, and then we would go off and do that operation, staying as long as there was material we felt worth obtaining.

On one occasion I worked with Major Keating. The message came through that there was a large tank battle going on and Keating decided it would be a good thing to go and have a look. As we were leaving Army HQ a war correspondent came up and asked if he could tag along. Keating replied: 'Yes, certainly, old man – join the fun.' Off we went to join the tank battle and Keating literally drove up amongst the tanks, parked behind one, and while I proceeded to film he began taking stills.

Suddenly, I heard a strange noise, a kind of whirring sound. I turned to Keating and said: 'What the hell's that?' 'Oh,' he replied, 'don't worry, that's just solid shot passing overhead. As long as it doesn't hit you you're all right.' I turned round to see where the war correspondent was and we saw a shady figure disappearing down the hillside towards his jeep and Army HQ.

One of the more intriguing – and controversial – Army Film and Photographic units operating in North Africa was Chet's Circus. A team of cameramen led by ex-Fleet Street photographer Sergeant Len Chetwyn they ranged over the rear areas producing convincing reconstructions of battle scenes. These well-shot photographs were taken up by the War Office as being excellent material for home consumption. Other photographers working in North Africa had mixed feelings about Chet's Circus. Stanley Gladstone emphasized the distinctions between the ordinary photographer and those from Fleet Street where reconstructions were commonplace: 'I regarded it as my job to try and get actual reality on to paper and not dream up what it might have been like.'

Although Billy Jordan accepted that there was a place for reconstructions at certain times, largely for continuity reasons in feature films, he didn't approve of its wholesale use:

I never staged a single thing in the desert. Not for any reason of principle but simply that I never had a chance to stage anything. I believe Chetwyn was given a free hand to operate as a mobile unit, staging his various actions where he could, using whatever troops were available. He was using cooks, bottle washers or whoever was back at base, and staging stuff that was reckoned to be real battle material with smoke and a few bangs let off with gun cotton. I think this was wrong as quite a number of members of the Unit were up at the front sticking their necks out trying to get real action pictures, and getting back reports from London asking for better action.

Peter Hopkinson recalls the pressure on the photographers to come up

Fleet Street's finest: the men of Chet's Circus adopt a suitably unmilitary pose; from left, Sergeants Jim Mapham (Leicester Mercury), John Herbert (Kodak), Chris Windows (Paramount), Len Chetwyn (Keystone) and Driver Sampey (Manchester Corporation Bus Depot). (E.20109)

with exciting material for public consumption and how it affected he way the Unit was run:

Geoffrey [Keating] only went along with re-enactment because I think he was being bombarded by the War Office, saying 'Where are the pictures of this great war?' But war isn't like the Hollywood concept wanted by our lords and masters, never was and never will be.

Looking back I suppose it's a pity that one of the most famous photographs of the Western Desert is a fake – one of Chetwyn's – of a guy storming a strongpoint, which in point of fact was made outside a cookhouse of the Australian Division's rear headquarters. It's phoney but it's a marvellous photograph.

Sergeant Chetwyn and his team were not the only cameramen who re-jigged history for the sake of audience expectations. Rex Keating worked with a number of cameramen, including the veteran Australian Frank Hurley, who photographed Shackleton's early polar expeditions. Keating explains Hurley's approach to war footage which provided a fair summary of the war photographer's dilemma:

Frank was a very good cameraman and he always turned in battle scenes which were remarkable. However, you must understand that a tank battle can cover

Chetwyn's famous/infamous photograph of Australians storming a cookhouse at rear headquarters. Over the years it has become the definitive Alamein photograph, gracing many book and magazine covers, and accompanied by suitably valiant captions. Another well-framed Chetwyn reconstruction is the front cover of this book, and even though it is not a genuine action photograph it none the less remains an excellent evocation of the Desert War. (E.18908)

Another classic Chetwyn picture of a tank recovery crew diving for cover while ostensibly under heavy fire. Like many of Chetwyn's compositions it has all the drama that real war photographs almost invariably lack: it is well framed and depicts the machines of war with men reacting to the sudden intrusion of combat, in this case a perfectly placed explosion. (E.13083)

many square miles of territory and often all you see is a puff of smoke on the horizon. The chances of you being able to point your camera at one of these incidents at that particular moment are thousands to one against.

Frank's argument was that the war was going on and people were being killed, so we had to give the public some indication of people really being killed and of tanks really being blown up. So behind the lines he would persuade the Army to set up, for example, two or three damaged tanks and place charges inside them. At the right moment the camera would then be pointing at the spot when the explosion took place. We argued the ethics of this a number of times and he always insisted that you had to show people what was going on even though you couldn't really do it in a tank battle. In the end I suppose I came to agree with him.

Private Armies

'The desert was a small raider's paradise,' wrote General Sir John Hackett after the war. Commando units had first been raised in Britain in the wake of the German conquest of continental Europe in 1940, mainly as a means of getting back at the Germans in some way, no matter how small. But it was in the Middle East that these disparate bands developed – encouraged by Wavell and Auchinleck – into the 'private armies' which swarmed across the desert in such profusion.

Their basic philosophy was that well-trained and highly motivated men could carry out specific missions impossible for conventional troops. The private armies reflected the British enthusiasm for the Boy's Own school of warfare, where derring-do by a resolute officer and his faithful band of men would win the day against vastly superior odds.

One private army universally acknowledged to be an elite force was the brainchild of a British officer, Major Ralph Bagnold, who had explored the Western Desert extensively in the inter-war years. He suggested to GHQ in Cairo the idea of setting up a deep reconnaissance unit capable of operating far behind enemy lines. Bagnold relates how he got permission to raise the Force which was to become the Long Range Desert Group (LRDG):

When the Italians declared war I took my courage in my hands and asked a friend of mine to send a note to the Commander-in-Chief. Within an hour I was sent for by Wavell and I told him that we needed a small mobile force able to penetrate the desert to the west of Egypt to see what was going on. Wavell said: 'What if you find the Italians are not doing anything in the interior at all?'

I said without thinking: 'How about some piracy on the high desert?'

At this his rather stern face broke into a grin, and he said:

'Can you be ready in six weeks?'

I replied: 'Yes, provided . . .'

'Yes, I know,' he interrupted, 'there'll be opposition and delay.'

He then rang his bell and a lieutenant-general came in as the chief of staff. Wavell said: 'Bagnold seeks a talisman. Get this typed out and I'll sign it straightaway: "I wish that any request made by Major Bagnold in person should be met instantly and without question."'

And it was like a talisman. I had complete *carte blanche* to do anything I liked.

Within six weeks we'd got together a volunteer force of New Zealanders. The New Zealand Division had arrived in Egypt but had yet to be supplied with arms and equipment because of shipping losses. So they were at a loose end. Apart from that, I wanted responsible volunteers who knew how to look after and maintain things, rather than the ordinary British Tommy who was apt to be wasteful. They were a marvellous lot of people, mostly sheep farmers who'd had fleets of trucks of their own and were used to looking after them.

Above: The vastness of the
desert can be appreciated in
this view of an LRDG patrol
taking a break deep in the
Sahara. (E.12385)

Right: A Chevrolet four-
wheel-drive truck of the
LRDG slips down the side of
a sand hill. Armament
comprises a Boyes anti-tank
rifle and a pintle-mounted
Lewis light machine-gun
operated by the front
passenger. (E.2298)

James Patch, a gunner in the Royal Artillery who subsequently joined the LRDG, explains how Bagnold extended his original recruitment policy:

As he'd taken a rather large number of New Zealanders he was made to cast around for other people and the next lot he chose were the Rhodesians who had a similar sort of background and were very inventive. After that he recruited from the Guards Brigade, who came from a very different background but were tip-top soldiers with a lot of self-discipline instilled into them. And they worked out very well too. Having chosen the guardsmen he looked further until he came to the yeomanry regiments of the British Army.

These different contingents were divided into separate 'lettered' patrols: S Patrol (Southern Rhodesians), G Patrol (Guards) and Y Patrol (Yeomanry). One of the Y Patrol recruits, F. G. Harrison, remembers Bagnold's words to him during his interview for the LRDG: 'I've got a very difficult job for you, most difficult. You must forget everything the Army ever taught you and learn to use your own initiative.' Roderick Matthews, another Y Patrol member, noted that 'you had to be a reasonable sort of type who could get on with people, someone who could live with twenty-odd blokes in fairly harsh conditions. You had to be fairly adaptable and have a certain amount of self-discipline.' F. G. Harrison explained how the LRDG's informal system of discipline worked in practice:

We never had parades or rifle inspections, like we'd been used to in the Army. Your common sense told you to keep your gun clean, one day you might want to use the damn thing. No one pulled rank, either. When dinner was served at night, the cook would shout 'Grub up!' and you got in the queue. If you were in front of an officer, there was none of this, 'I'm an officer, therefore I go first' business. We were a very democratic unit, and it worked very well.

Driving modified Chevrolet and Ford 30-cwt trucks the LRDG operated from a string of oases deep in the desert, sending out patrols throughout Libya to as far west as the border with Tunisia. In an unconventional unit like the LRDG, new methods and modes of operation developed. Bagnold:

The creation of a completely unorthodox force in six weeks was quite a feat. And it was great fun. There was an awful lot to do. Everything was new. Clothing and footwear had to be redesigned. Army boots were no good at all because they got filled with sand. So I had sandals made – the Indian North-West Frontier chappali which was very tough with an open toe so that if sand got into it you could shoot it out with a kick.

All we wore was a shirt and shorts and Arab headgear. The advantage of wearing a shemagh or shawl which goes round the head, was that it flaps in the wind and keeps the face cool. In a sandstorm – when the sand drives unmercifully against your face – you just wrapped the headdress round to protect your cheek. The men took to it at once; they realized it was so much better. But because of the need for security we thought it unsafe to put out a contract in Egypt for 200 Arab headdresses. Consequently we got them off the Palestine Police stores.

LRDG soldiers engaged in one of their prime missions – recording enemy troop and vehicle movement along the coast road. (E.12434)

Bagnold's flair for unconventional solutions to desert conditions included the sun compass (*see* page 30) and a radiator overflow condensor. Harrison explains how it worked:

We had this wonderful means of conserving water from the radiator. When the water boiled, instead of it being lost through the overflow pipe, it was blown off into a can on the side of the truck which was half full of water where it would condense. When the engine cooled it would be sucked back into the radiator again. If everything was right and there were no leaks you could go the whole life of a lorry and never put any more water in after the first filling.

Water conservation was obviously important at the personal level. For seasoned desert hands like Bagnold this presented few difficulties:

We had a water ration of three pints in winter and four in summer. It was really enough if one was careful and lived at the bottom of one's spare gallon of water, instead of at the top like most people. Everybody has a spare gallon of water in their bodies. Most people in hot weather want to drink and they overdrink. They perspire freely and waste water which does no good and doesn't cool you at all. But if you keep to the bottom of the spare gallon your perspiration only moistens the skin to provide evaporation and cooling. If you don't sweat so much you don't lose salt. We had no trouble with lack of salt whereas on the coast they did.

Medical officer to L Detachment of the SAS, Captain M. J. Pleydell was aware of the psychological aspects of water conservation:

A mixed group of weatherbeaten LRDG men brew up during a pause in a desert patrol. (E.2305)

Water discipline was essential as supplies were sometimes very limited. You could eke out your water bottle in sips, or drink it in gulps. In either case the sound of someone else drinking could cause envy and fray the temper. The adjustment to water discipline was largely psychological, and had nothing to do with the size of the individual.

Patches of soft sand were a minor hazard and they slowed progress through the desert. Bagnold again had a solution to the problem:

If one was bogged down the nose of the car would tip right forward, axle deep in the sand. The problem was to get it out. Going round the junk shops in the slums of Cairo we found these heavy metal channels which had originally been used in the First World War for roofing dugouts. They were about five feet long and you could carry one under each arm, just. You scooped the sand away from the back wheels and pushed the channel under the wheel. Directly it gripped the car would be shoved forward and hopefully you'd get out of the soft patch on to harder ground.

During the Second World War every vehicle in the Army was equipped with these sand channels, which they had made for them. I had first used them successfully as far back as 1927.

The professionalism of the LRDG compared favourably with most other private armies, which in the main were organized and led by inspired amateurs. The commandos were the most famous of these military improvisations. Under the command of Colonel Robert

Laycock, 8 and 11 Commando – for a time known as Layforce – had been despatched to the Middle East but there they experienced mixed fortunes.

Terence Frost had been posted to Palestine as a trooper in a yeomanry regiment but feeling isolated from the rest of the war he was only too keen to answer the call for special duties:

It seemed that the war was never going to reach us and so I volunteered to go to the commandos because one wanted to get some action. Once in the commandos the training was very different for me having come from the territorials. Also I didn't know that the volunteers from the regulars hadn't actually volunteered at all. They had been kicked out for getting drunk or socking the sergeant major and I had the shock of my life when I found this out. I was amongst a real tough shower of blokes who were actually marvellous once you got to know them. But they scared the pants off you the way they lived.

Once the commandos in the Middle East had been organized and trained the next step was to find them a suitable role to play. Amphibious operations were their designated area of responsiblity and their first opportunity for action was a raid on Axis positions around the port of Bardia on the night of 19/20 April 1941. The second-in-command of one of the commando troops gives his account of the raid:

The operation depended on the Navy putting us ashore on a pitch dark night on four separate beaches near Bardia. Our troop landed just after midnight and our objective was to blow up one of our munition dumps left at Bardia after our troops were driven out. We were in light raiding order, which meant that we carried almost no equipment, just weapons and hand grenades.

The Navy got us ashore although we were all soaked because the assault landing craft found it difficult to get close in. There was some machine-gun fire about five minutes after we came ashore and we were delayed by the unexpected presence of a steep-sided wadi which we had to clamber up.

The men got to the top and then made straight for a German laager – which contained an advanced repair depot for a German armoured unit as well as our old munition dumps. In the pitch dark we set it alight. There were explosions all round now, especially where the other troops had landed on Bardia beach and were getting rid of the harbour bridge and the vital water installations in the port.

We were running behind time, and if we wanted to be picked up by the landing craft, it seemed that it might be as well to start back. At length we got to a point on the cliff above the beach, and slid the men down. After about half an hour an assault landing craft came in but only had room for ten people. I rather doubted whether they could send in another boat for us as the weather was turning nasty.

Those of us who had to stay behind divided into three small parties. We holed up in some caves in the nearby cliffs as day broke. However, the Germans had been looking for us the whole morning and eventually spotted us. We had to surrender. Afterwards we were taken to Rommel's HQ which was nearby, and there he told us we were 'very foolish but very brave'.

A partial success, the Bardia raid was followed by others, notably the Keyes raid of November 1941. Intended to kill Rommel at his HQ the

Lieutenant-Colonel Geoffrey Keyes. At only 24 he was the youngest soldier to hold this rank in the British Army, only to be killed in the abortive raid on Rommel's HQ. (E.4732)

operation was a complete failure and Lieutenant-Colonel Geoffrey Keyes who led the raid was killed instead (receiving a posthumous VC for his courage and leadership). Faulty intelligence and desperately over-optimistic planning had doomed the attempt from the outset.

The major problem with these commando raids was that they were too large and far too ambitious. More successful were those ventures which were modest in scope and scale, where resources were carefully matched to a specific task.

James Sherwood provides an example of the economical approach to special operations. While in training in Scotland with 8 Commando he had transferred to the folbot section, troops given special training in canoes (folbots) and small-scale amphibious operations. Sherwood and the folbot section were sent to the Middle East to join Layforce but after its disbandment the section was transformed into the Special Boat Section (the forerunner of the Special Boat Squadron). Based in Alexandria the SBS was ferried around in Royal Navy submarines:

Our operations involved carrying out reconnaissance of some particular area or coast or putting agents ashore on to Crete or mainland Greece. The agents all took wireless sets and explosives and money, all done up in biscuit tins. One operation involved a night landing of a Greek on the Plain of Marathon. The chap hopped into the canoe wearing an ordinary burberry-type raincoat, soft grcy felt hat, collar and tie – just as though he was going on a shopping expedition into town.

There was a large German outpost about half a mile from our landing point which we had identified through the submarine periscope during the day. Fortunately as we paddled the mile or so from the submarine to the shore we didn't bump into any German patrols. We had a dark night and a fairly calm sea. We landed on the beach and out he stepped as if he were getting out of a pleasure rowboat at a seaside resort. He unloaded the gear and then just vanished.

Recovering from injuries a young commando officer, Lieutenant David Stirling, decided that there was a place for small raiding teams to be parachuted behind enemy lines. Supported by Generals Ritchie and Auchinleck, Stirling was given the go-ahead and in mid-1941 he began recruiting volunteers from the remains of Layforce. Stirling and his sixty-five recruits gave themselves the title L Detachment Special Air Service Brigade, intended to deceive German intelligence into thinking there was a new airborne brigade being formed in the Middle East.

The first mission for the SAS was a parachute attack on two enemy airfields on 16 November 1941, but the men were dispersed by high winds and the whole affair was a fiasco, the detachment losing 70 per cent of its strength. The survivors were picked up by the LRDG. Stirling saw the effectiveness of their operation and immediately abandoned the parachute concept in favour of overland operations in heavily armed jeeps guided to their targets by the LRDG.

Specializing in attacks against enemy airfields the SAS achieved some excellent results. On one occasion the SAS second in command, Paddy Mayne, led a raid which destroyed forty Italian aircraft. Promoted to major, Stirling was allowed to expand his force, which attracted a stream of recruits, incorporating such diverse elements as French paratroops, the SBS (albeit reluctantly), the Greek Sacred Squadron and the Special Interrogation Group, comprising German-speaking ex-nationals strongly opposed to fascism.

Captain Pleydell, the SAS medical officer, found membership of this unusual organization an interesting change from more conventional duties. Pleydell remembers:

Although life was free and easy in the mess, discipline was required for exercises and operations. On the operations in which I was involved, our patrol would make long detours south of the battle line and then loop up north to within striking distance of an airfield or similar target. Camouflage had to be expert, so that when you hid up you couldn't be detected – even at close distance. Slow flying enemy aircraft could follow our tracks to our hiding places and they represented a real threat. It was a hit-and-run, hide-and-seek type of war.

Working alongside the more organized of the private armies were individuals engaged in undercover work behind enemy lines in Libya. Vladimir Peniakoff was a Russo-Belgian who after service in the French Army in the First World War had worked in Egypt as an engineer in a sugar factory. Securing a commission in the British Army, Peniakoff –

nicknamed 'Popski' – embraced the idea of special operations with
complete enthusiasm. Initially he worked with Libyan Arabs hostile to
the Axis but with LRDG help he expanded his organization and went
over to mounting sabotage raids on Axis positions. One of the most
successful involved the destruction of 100,000 gallons of Axis petrol.

The great German victories in June and July of 1942 made it imperative that the private armies strike at the Axis, especially since enemy lines
of communication were now stretched from Tripoli to Alamein, making
them vulnerable to attack. At the same time the private armies had been
growing in numbers, size and confidence. The time seemed ripe to
combine their skills and experience in a big raid that would shock the
all-conquering Axis forces. Along with the SAS, SBS and LRDG
(acting as 'taxi-drivers') were units of Commandos, Royal Marines and
regular infantry, plus support from the Navy and the RAF. The basic
plan was to make simultaneous attacks on Tobruk and Benghazi (with a
subsidiary raid on Barce) from both land and sea.

Launched on 13 September 1942 it was a total failure, the various
British forces suffering heavy casualties for no gain – the Navy lost two
destroyers and an AA cruiser as well as numerous smaller craft. The
root cause was the old problem of having too many over-ambitious
objectives, which relied on good fortune for success. Compounding the

Colonel David Stirling,
founder of the SAS, stands by
one of his jeep-mounted
patrols. Bristling with Vickers
and Browning machine-guns,
the jeeps are loaded with
spare jerricans (captured
from the Germans – hence
their name) and fitted with
the water condensers (at front
of jeep) developed by
Bagnold. (E.21338)

An SAS officer wearing typical desert garb, including North-West Frontier chappali sandals. (E.21344)

disaster was the poor security surrounding the whole operation; Axis intelligence was fairly certain of the objectives and time of the attack, thus all surprise was lost.

James Sherwood of the SBS was on the raid as part of the SAS column assigned to attack Benghazi. After travelling across the desert to the forward oasis of Kufra they set off for Benghazi:

We discovered our role. While the SAS went about their part of the exercise in keeping Benghazi occupied, we were to assemble our canoes on the side of the harbour, paddle out with limpet mines and try to sink enemy ships there. Nobody was enthusiastic about the plan, and a great deal of moaning and grumbling went on.

We arrived late but for better or worse David Stirling decided the operation would carry on. We drove down the escarpment to Benghazi with headlights full on, Stirling's idea being to bluff the enemy that no British force would dream of driving with their lights on so close to the enemy. After finding a proper track we came to a striped frontier pole directly ahead of us. I remember Stirling getting out of his jeep and walking up to the post quite casually to see what was going on. He was a very brave bloke. Instead of just ordinary Italian guards being there – which we had expected – the whole operation was blown and the Germans were there waiting for us.

They opened up on us with everything they'd got. We were told to get out of it, every man for himself. There was terrible confusion as the jeeps and lorries tried to turn round. I saw shot and stuff flying all over the place. The extraordinary thing was that the enemy scored very few hits which was just as well as we were sitting on top of our explosives and if we'd been hit the SBS would have disappeared in a big bang. A jeep was hit in the petrol tank and went up in flames, which added to the already over-illuminated scene. We headed out of it, having achieved nothing at all.

After a dramatic escape through the mountains of the Djebel Ahkdar the SAS/SBS column managed to escape back to the relative safety of the desert. On the amphibious side of the raid the disaster was greater still. D. Jermain was an experienced motor torpedo boat (MTB) commander involved in supporting the attack on Tobruk. As at Benghazi, confusion reigned:

It was with much surprise that at first light I saw *Sikh* and *Zulu* close to the coast under overwhelming fire from shore batteries [both these destroyers were subsequently sunk]. I had never been advised that they were participating, a recipe for disorder.

By the time the sun was up it was obvious that we had walked into a trap and the only thing to do was to disengage. I gathered up some boats and was making to seaward when a small biplane began attacking us before we were able to assume our well-tried diamond-shaped defensive formation. After picking off two or three boats, some of which still had fuel in cans on deck, the fighter turned on me. My tactic of turning towards and going full-speed ahead to force the plane into a dangerously steep dive worked for three runs. But eventually he managed to come up from astern and his bullets were running up my wake to within a few feet when he ran out of ammunition. He then flew parallel, waggled his wings and went home after a courageous and successful sortie.

A group of the Fighting
French SAS meets up with
local Arabs during the drive
to Tripoli after the victory at
Alamein. (NA.674)

I collected my boats and set off seaward for twenty miles, which experience showed to be the limit for fighters, and thence to Alexandria under frequent attack by dive bombers.

One consequence of the Benghazi–Tobruk disaster was the appointment of John Hackett to act as a liaison officer between the High Command and the private armies. Initially reluctant to leave his regimental duties he found them a 'very varied list of prima donnas. My job was to try and make special operations comprehensible and palatable to senior officers, which took a lot of doing because they were not an easy lot to keep under full control.' Once Hackett had assessed the motley crew he was working with he set about trying to improve inter-'army' co-operation:

One of the chief problems was to keep the little armies out of each other's way. The Long Range Desert Group would be practising its infinitely careful reconnaissance, where, for example, two men with binoculars and a wireless set would list every vehicle travelling on the coast road between Tripoli and Tunis, reporting back to GHQ every night. A beautiful operation. Then the SAS would come around and blow up some aeroplanes but they were very careless about things and they'd leave a lot lying around. They would stir things up no end and out would come the Axis forces and they would find the LRDG. This

199

had to be prevented so I had to draw a line down the map like a medieval pope separating the Spanish from the Portuguese, saying 'west of this, LRDG only; east of this, SAS only.' That kept them more or less out of each other's hair.

Another task for Hackett was to get Popski's operation going again after Tobruk. A suitable name for the group remained a problem: 'They were given the pompous title of No. 1 Long Range Demolition Squadron but that was only to get outsiders to take it seriously.' The title was considered to be too cumbersome for everyday use and Hackett, Popski and other officers discussed an alternative: 'We argued about this for some time and finally I said, "We're wasting a lot of time so unless anyone else can think of a suitable name, I'm going to call you Popski's Private Army and have done with it." "Done!" said Popski.'

Unlike his predecessors, Montgomery did not have a very high opinion of the private armies. In particular he was not keen on having his best men and NCOs poached by the SAS. Hackett and David Stirling secured an appointment with the Eighth Army commander at his HQ at Bourg al Arab just prior to the Alamein battle. Hackett recalls that Montgomery was not impressed by their entreaties to secure volunteers for the SAS. Montgomery replied:

'What makes you think, Stirling, that these men will fight better under your command than under mine. And, anyway, they won't be ready for the battle [Alamein].'

I couldn't resist saying, 'Well, they may not be trained in time for the next battle but they will be trained for the one after that and the battles to follow.'

This was too much for Monty. He hammered the map at Alamein and said, 'There will be no other battle in Africa. This is going to be the last battle. My mandate is to destroy Rommel, and I propose to destroy him,' he said tapping the Alamein position, 'just here.'

David, who was never well known for his obsequiousness, said: 'Oh yes, General, but the last general told us something like that, and the one before him too.'

We didn't get any recruits, you won't be surprised to hear.

In the follow-up to Alamein the private armies were highly successful in harrying the retreating Axis forces until the fighting bogged down in Tunisia. With the end of the war in Africa in May 1943 some of the private armies were disbanded while others went on to find new roles in other theatres of war.

Since 1945 a small publishing industry has grown up glorifying the private armies (and their successors in the postwar period). Certainly, their exploits make exciting reading but in the sober light of military accounting the debit ledger looms large. Although the LRDG and to a large degree the SAS fall outside this criticism, too many good officers and men and too large a quantity of scarce resources were wasted on hare-brained schemes of dubious worth.

Postscript
From Tripoli to Tunis

The Torch landings of 8 November 1942 transformed the war in North Africa. A combined Anglo-American operation, Torch consisted of three major amphibious landings in Morocco, Oran and Algiers. The Vichy French government (an ostensible ally of Germany) still maintained direct control over Morocco, Algeria and Tunisia but there were strong anti-German feelings within the colonial administration which the Allies were able to exploit. This ensured that opposition to the amphibious invasion was confused and ineffectual. Once ashore the Allies suppressed what remained of Vichy French opposition. They then drove eastwards towards Tunisia in the hope of cutting off Rommel's forces retreating back through Libya after their defeat at Alamein.

Although Torch caught the Germans by surprise they were quick to respond. Hitler had determined that North Africa must be held at all costs and reinforcements were rushed to Tunisia, as the advance guard of the 5th Panzer Army under the command of Colonel-General Hans-Jürgen von Arnim. As a result the Allied push on Tunis was thwarted. By the end of November mobile operations had come to a close and the Allies were forced to prepare for a full-scale offensive which would have to wait until the new year.

The mountainous terrain and poor weather made conditions difficult for the Allied advance but more complex still were the problems of command. This was the first instance of combined operations between Britain and the United States. Fortunately, despite differing strategic priorities and military systems, both nations generally worked well together – a blueprint for the future.

More ambiguous was the position of the French in North Africa. Despite initial reservations they were won over to the Allied cause (especially now that Germany looked like losing the war) and after some uncertainty their forces were integrated into the Allied command structure. General Dwight Eisenhower was appointed Supreme Allied Commander although tactical matters came under the control of British commanders: General Alexander moved up from Cairo to take charge of 18th Army Group while Lieutenant-General K. A. N. Anderson led the First Army, a multinational force of British, American and French troops.

Meanwhile, Rommel had been conducting a well-ordered retreat across Libya, vacating Tripoli on 22 January 1943 in order to take up a defensible position on the Mareth Line just inside Tunisia. The Eighth Army advanced steadily behind the Germans, crossing the Tunisian border on 4 February and building up supplies in anticipation of a set-piece attack on the Mareth Line.

Before the Allies were ready to mount their offensive the Germans struck. On 14 February German armoured columns forced their way across the mountains and routed the inexperienced US II Corps in front of the Kasserine pass. The German commanders, however, failed to exploit their success; Allied reserves were rushed to the threatened area and the line held. A second Axis attack was mounted against the Eighth Army opposite the Mareth Line at Medenine on 6 March, but it was a clumsy affair and, well-armed with anti-tank guns, the desert veterans repulsed the assault, inflicting heavy German tank losses. Exhausted and frustrated, Rommel left Africa for good three days later, passing control of German forces to von Arnim.

Montgomery's action against the fortified Mareth Line got under way on 20 March. The basic plan called for a major blow on the centre-right with a wide outflanking move on the left carried out by the New Zealand Corps (the original division augmented by additional troops), intended to draw away reserves from the main battle. A well-timed counter attack by the XV Panzer Division, however, stalled the main British attack so that Montgomery switched the focus of the assault, despatching the 1st Armoured Division in support of the New Zealanders' 'left hook'. Battered by a ferocious assault from the Desert Air Force and fearing encirclement the Axis forces adroitly withdrew from Mareth to a new position at Wadi Akarit, although the panzer divisions had lost much of their armour in the battle.

Montgomery launched a frontal assault against the Wadi Akarit defences on the night of 6/7 April, forcing a breach in the Axis line. Faced by a new threat on his right flank from the rejuvenated US II Corps (now under General George Patton) the Axis commander, General Giovanni Messe, decided against continuing the fight and withdrew northward toward Enfidaville. The Axis forces were now constrained within a perimeter surrounding the ports of Bizerta and Tunis.

While the Eighth Army advanced from the south, the First Army began its offensive from the west. On 22 April the British V and IX Corps struck in the centre while the US II Corps attacked along the coast. The Axis troops held on desperately to their mountain defences, especially on Longstop Hill where the British 78th Division fought a long four-day battle to wrest control from the Germans. As the Eighth Army's attack against Enfidaville had stalled, Montgomery despatched troops to support the First Army offensive which had yet to break out of the mountains.

During the first week in May Allied units began to push forward on to the coastal plain: on 5 May the British 1st Infantry Division captured Djebel Bou Aoukaz and the following day the 4th Indian Division cleared the Axis off the key Medjez el Bab position. The way was open for exploitation by the tanks and on 7 May the 7th Armoured Division – the original Desert Rats – swept triumphantly into Tunis. Further north the Americans captured Bizerta, leaving the Axis to make a last stand on the Cape Bon peninsula. But the Allied breakthrough had overwhelmed the Axis command which was unable to organize effective resistance. On 12 May von Arnim was captured and a day later Messe formally surrendered what was left of the Axis armies.

Hitler's reckless policy of massively reinforcing the Tunisian bridge-head bore bitter fruit, for along with 115,000 Italians he lost 125,000 German troops to the POW camps. The vast haul of Axis prisoners was a special bonus for the British who for nearly three years had fought over desert and mountain for this moment. On 13 May Alexander sent this laconic despatch to Churchill in London: 'Sir, it is my duty to report that the campaign in Tunisia is over. All enemy resistance has ceased. We are masters of the North African shores.'

Jubilant British troops drive through the streets of Tunis, 8 May 1943. A few days later the war in North Africa would finally be over. (NA.2560)

Index of Contributors

This index is designed to list those individuals whose memoirs, diaries, papers and reminiscences have been quoted in the book. Also, it acknowledges the permission given by the copyright holders to use the material housed within the Imperial War Museum; their names appear in brackets after those of the contributor they are associated with. Every effort has been made to trace the copyright holders and the Museum would be grateful for any information which might help locate those whose identities or addresses are not known.

Department of Documents

Lieutenant-Colonel J. Anderson Smith (Mrs G. A. Williamson) 160–61; Captain G. C. Blundell RN 81–2, 87, 90–91; Mr V. L. Bosazza 161; Mr R. L. Braithwaite 23, 117; Major-General R. Briggs (Mrs N. R. Edwards) 171; Mr J. E. Brooks 137; Mr L. Challoner 72, 158; Mr F. B. Coombes 84–5; Major R. H. Dahl 29, 54, 139; Brigadier R. B. T. Daniell 25; Lord Deramore [Richard de Yarburgh-Bateson] 144–5; Group Captain G. V. Howard (F. G. Travers) 143; Captain D. Jermain RN 198–9; Mr J. W. Kelly 22, 25, 26; Lieutenant-Commander J. B. Lamb RN (Mrs Lamb/Mr Simon Lamb) 13–14, 14, 82–4, 122; Lieutenant D. A. Main 39, 68, 169–70, 173–4; Major-General C. H. Miller (Major L. Melzer) 47–8, 126–7; Field Marshal Viscount Montgomery of Alamein 157; Mr K. W. Morris 63, 68, 72–3, 178; Lieutenant-Colonel M. E. Parker 58; Major D. F. Parry 60, 100; Captain M. J. Pleydell 45, 49, 50–51, 51, 193, 196; Mr E. Randolph 44; Dt T. Stephanides (Mrs Alexia Mercouris) 9, 10–11, 14, 15, 48, 74, 113, 146–7; Flying Officer G. A. Stillingfleet 34; Mr H. L. Sykes 22, 25, 27, 31, 55, 120, 164; Colonel F. M. V. Tregear 110, 111, 139; Mr L. E. Tutt 3, 5, 17, 21, 24–5, 26–7, 27–8, 37, 39, 63, 66, 71, 134, 135; Mr H. A. Wilson 41, 72; Major-General D. N. Wimberley (Mrs M. Wimberley) 130, 133–4, 135, 161–3, 163–4, 166; Mr J. H. Witte 71–2.

Department of Sound Records

Major R. A. Bagnold 189, 191, 192, 193; Captain Barker* 10; Captain O. Bird* 110; Lieutenant-Colonel R. Bromley-Gardner 30, 75, 103; Sergeant Covell* 166; Major R. Crisp* 175; Mr H. Daniel 66; Mr J. H. Daniel 21, 27, 28, 62, 131; Major-General A. H. G. Dobson 102, 117, 123; Mr L. Durrell 74, 75; Mr H. Fitzjohn 41, 42, 68, 70, 76, 77, 97, 104–05, 124–5, 125; Major-General H. R. B. Foote 106; Mr J. M. R. Frazer 55, 61; Mr T. Frost 194; Mr F. G. Gillard 179; Mr S. Gladstone 183, 184; Mr J. V. Griffiths 132; General Sir John Hackett 96, 102, 102–03, 189, 199–200, 200; Mr H. Harper 18, 97, 97–8, 127, 128, 131, 157–8, 164, 165; Mr J. G. Harris, 35, 36–7, 174; Mr F. G. Harrison 51, 191, 192; Mr C. Hayes 31; Mr R. Hill 177–8; Mr P. Hopkinson 183, 185; Mr F. C. Jones 62, 76; Mr R. A. Joynes 48; Mr W. Jordan 184; Mr R. Keating 9, 13, 75, 179, 185, 188; Mr R. H. Kitson 122–3; Mr F. R. Knowles 131; Mr J. E. Longstaff 37, 50; Sergeant Maile* 166–9; Mr B. H. Martin 110, 123–4; Mr

R. C. Mathews 51, 191; Mr A. H. McGee 37, 40; Mr E. Norris 160; General Sir Richard O'Connor 2, 4, 12, 13, 16; Mr J. D. Patch 29, 191; Lieutenant Pompei* 148; Major-General N. C. Rogers 26; Air Chief Marshal Sir Frederick Rosier 142, 143, 148, 149–50, 153; Mr H. Sell 31, 35, 35–6, 37, 39–40, 77, 106–07, 108–09, 112, 117, 119–20; Mr J. B. B. Sherwood 195–6, 198; Mr G. Talbot 63, 172, 180–81, 181–2, 182; Flight Lieutenant Wallace* 151–3; Mr E. Ward* 86–7, 150; Mr W. I. Watson 107, 109, 120, 173; Mr C. Wilmot* 12. Anonymous recordings: Australian sergeant at Tobruk* 18; British sergeant major at Tobruk* 19; Commando officer on Bardia raid 194; South African armoured car trooper* 58; South African fighter squadron CO* 145–6.

*Transcriptions of contemporary BBC sound recordings – by permission of the British Broadcasting Corporation.

Australian War Memorial

The majority of Australian material has come from the Australian War Memorial (GPO Box 345, Canberra ACT 2601); the book has greatly benefited from this UK–Australian co-operation. The author would particularly like to thank Dr Peter Londey (Acting Head, Historical Research) along with Stephen Allen, Judy Crabb, Anne-Marie Conde and Historical Research Section and Research Centre staff at the Australian War Memorial.

Major Ballerstedt (AWM 92, 3DRL 2632/37, Tobruk – Translations of German Diaries and Documents) 136; Major D. J. Benjamin/ Sergeant J. R. Oates (AWM 54, Item 523/7/16 – Discipline at Tobruk) 135; Lieutenant J. Dewhurst (AWM 54, Item 523/7/16 – Canteen Activities at Tobruk) 25; Major-General C. H. Finlay (Transcript of interview with Charles Hector Finlay, Major-General RL, 24 June 1990. Interview S941, The Keith Murdoch Sound Archive of Australia in the war of 1939–45) 113–14, 131; Wing Commander R. H. Gibbes (Transcript of interview with Wing Commander R. H. (Bobby) Gibbes, 3 Squadron RAAF, 28 April 1990, Interview S938, The Keith Murdoch Sound Archive) 143, 148; Corporal R. L. Hoffman (AWM 52, Item 8/2/16, War Diary, HQ 16 Australian Infantry Brigade) 6, 8, 14; Squadron Leader P. Jeffrey (Transcript of interview with Peter Jeffrey, 3 Squadron RAAF, 2 July 1990. Interview S951, The Keith Murdoch Sound Archive) 131, 142; Corporal V. Knight (Transcript of interview with Corporal Victor Knight, 2/2nd Machine-Gun Battalion, 17 March 1989. Interview S555, The Keith Murdoch Sound Archive) 114–15; Mr P. Loffman (Transcript of interview with Phil Loffman, 2/28th Battalion, April 1989. Interview S557, The Keith Murdoch Sound Archive) 125–6; Major-General I. G. Mackay (AWM 52, Item 8/2/16, War Diary, HQ 16 Australian Infantry Brigade) 14; Lieutenant-General Sir Leslie Morshead (AWM 92, 3DRL 2632/12, Papers of Lieutenant-General Sir Leslie Morshead) 133; Sergeant J. R. Oates (3DRL 2632/47, Reports on operations at El Alamein, July-November 1942) 158–60; Corporal H. Rawson (AWM 54, Item 521/2/1, First Battle of Bardia) 6; Mr M. Trigger (Transcript of interview with Maurice Trigger, 2/2nd Machine-Gun Battalion, 17 April 1989. Interview S591, The Keith Murdoch Sound Archive) 113.

Anonymous document: Australian Military History Section (AWM 54, Item 523/7/16 – Bush artillery at Tobruk) 22.

Index